# FACING THE CHALLENGE OF EMANCIPATION

# Facing the Challenge of Emancipation

A Study of the Ministry of William Hart Coleridge,
First Bishop of Barbados, 1824–1842

## Sehon S. Goodridge

### Edited by
### Anthony de Vere Phillips

*Canoe Press*
Jamaica • Barbados • Trinidad and Tobago

Barbados Museum & Historical Society

Canoe Press
7A Gibraltar Hall Road, Mona
Kingston 7, Jamaica
www.uwipress.com

The Barbados Museum and Historical Society
St Ann's Garrison,
St Michael, Barbados BB14038
www.barbmuse.org.bb

© 2014 by Janet Goodridge

All rights reserved. Published 2014

ISBN: 978-976-653-014-3 (print)

First published 1981, Cedar Press, Bridgetown, Barbados

*Cover illustrations*: The Right Reverend William Hart Coleridge, DD, Bishop of Barbados and the Leeward Islands, by an unknown artist (circa 1834). Courtesy of Sir Charles Cave, Bt, FRICS, Devon, England. Sketch of the Society for the Propagation of the Gospel chapel in Barbados by the Right Reverend William Hart Coleridge.

Cover and book design by Robert Harris
Set in Sabon 10.2/14.5 x 27
Printed in the United States of America.

# CONTENTS

Biographical Foreword: The Right Reverend
   Sehon S. Goodridge / vii
*Anthony De Vere Phillips*

Preface to the First Edition / xvii

1   The Colonial Church before 1824 / 1

2   First Bishop: His Role and Jurisdiction / 7

3   Places of Worship: Parish Churches, Chapels and Chapel Schools / 15

4   The Ministry: Administration, Recruitment and Theological Education / 28

5   Public Education: Integral to Amelioration and Evangelisation / 49

6   Pastoral Care and African Customs / 63

7   Social Reform: Gradual and Peaceful / 77

8   Return to England: Mission Accomplished / 87

Appendix I Building Funds: Source and Use / 95

Appendix II Clergy / 96

Appendix III Coleridge: Builder and Rebuilder / 98

Notes / 101

Bibliography / 115

Index / 119

# BIOGRAPHICAL FOREWORD

## THE RIGHT REVEREND SEHON S. GOODRIDGE

### ANTHONY DE VERE PHILLIPS

IN SOME LIBRARY CATALOGUES ONE is presented with a stark listing of the Sehon S. Goodridge items as *Facing the Challenge of Emancipation: A Study of the Ministry of William Hart Coleridge, First Bishop of Barbados, 1824–1842* (Bridgetown: Cedar Press, 1981), and *Facing the Challenge of Racism: Story, Reflection and Practice in Theological Education and Training* (London: Advisory Board of Ministry, in association with the Runnymede Trust, Ministry Paper No. 8, 1994). This is, in fact, an incomplete listing.[1] But Sehon Goodridge was definitely not one to decline a challenge. He saw the church as the watchman and guardian of society.

Goodridge completed a draft of the manuscript of his path-breaking study, *Facing the Challenge of Emancipation,* while on a Sabbatical leave from Codrington College, spent between three Oxford colleges: All Souls, Wolfson and Queen's. The book was published in 1981. It provided a clear analysis of how an old order, enslavement, gave way to a regime of freedom (with distinct boundaries).

Goodridge's focus was on the main agent, Bishop Coleridge of Barbados and the Leeward Islands. Bishop Coleridge was a decided moderniser. He saw that the economic context was being transformed and concluded that therefore the superstructure also had to undergo a fundamental shake-up. His extensive building programme of churches, chapels, and schools provided the visible signs of change. More importantly, the preaching and teaching inside those buildings aimed to create a new people. They, however, had to internalise the new ethos and the new culture.

Goodridge was convinced that there were lessons to be learned from the Coleridge innovations. He did not stop, but continued his intellectual search in an increasingly wide range of sources. Fortunately, this era was peculiarly well suited to Goodridge's quest. He turned out to be the right man in the right place at the right time.

Goodridge had a remarkably active career from the 1960s to the years of the twenty-first century until his retirement on 31 July 2005 owing to illness. He died on 28 December 2007, aged seventy years.

He was not one to stand idly by. He lived in an era of rapid change and kept pace with the momentum. He allied with the ecumenical and progressive trends of the era.

He was a regional and international activist. For example, he was drafted onto the Inter-Anglican Theological and Doctrinal Commission in 1981. This was a think tank consisting of fifteen distinguished theologians from all over the world. The second meeting was held in Barbados in 1983. The theologians were drawn from Hong Kong, New Zealand, Ireland, Brazil, Tanzania, Canada, Oxford, Ghana, Australia, South Africa and Sri Lanka. He was one of a cohort of international scholars. He had links to King's College London, two campuses of the University of the West Indies, Codrington College in Barbados, Oxford, Cambridge, and universities and colleges in the United States and Canada.

Goodridge developed in a watershed period, the end of the old era of imperialism and the onset of decolonisation. The record shows that in 1963 every bishop in the Caribbean was White and that most were expatriate. It was urged that local, Black leadership must be sought. It was agreed that it was necessary that some promising young Blacks be provided with opportunities to gain higher qualifications. On completion, they would be able to respond to the challenge of leadership.

Sehon Goodridge was identified and went on to King's College London to read for the Bachelor of Divinity degree. While in England, he married Janet, whom he had met in Barbados. Marriage added to the stability of his life.

Goodridge turned out to be the right man in the right place at the right time. The position of Anglican chaplain to the student body at the University of the West Indies, Mona, Jamaica was vacant and on graduation from King's College London he was invited to fill the post.

Let us hear from the man himself. Goodridge introduced himself as a full-blown creole personality:

> May I invite you to consider my own journey and exploration. I myself was formed to a great extent by British culture in the West Indies. Our British institutions were transplanted there. I sang 'Rule Britannia' and 'Land of Hope and Glory'! When I came to London I saw the Nelson, but we have the real Nelson in Barbados. The Anglican Church as part of that culture was a perfect transplant. The parochial system, pipe organ, 'Hymns Ancient and Modern', the lot. I sang hymns like 'He sends the snow in winter': I saw snow for the first time in 1965. I was nurtured in an Anglican family and sucked in Anglicanism like my mother's milk The British culture was also reflected in the nature and ethos of the whole education system. The missionaries had done a good job in education.

Later, he was to give a more detailed account of his development in mid-career:

> After further theological education in Britain, I returned to the Caribbean in the middle sixties and was fully immersed in the search for identity and the affirmation of our African retentions which were driven underground by the dominant British culture but were kept alive by certain rituals of what were called the arbour – wooden huts – the arbour institutions. I imagined my task as a theological educator as the questions were raised: 'Who is the Christ?' 'Is he a European Christ?' 'What about the Black Messiah?' 'Can we sing the Lord's song to the melody of our own voices?' To these questions of identity were added those of a new historical and anthropological consciousness. What value can be derived from our responsive histories as we write our own histories and history is no longer written about us? Has not the time come that we must see ourselves not only as the objects but the subjects of our own histories? Are we not a witness people? Should we not search for a new anthropology, in contrast to that old anthropology which advocated superiority, inferiority, civilised, heathen; that was an anthropology based upon certain set dichotomies? Surely we are no longer aliens and foreigners? This has implications not only for those others far away but also for those others in our British society.

Bishop Goodridge's career may conveniently be summarised as being a series of responses to successive challenges:

- The challenge of preaching and teaching
- The challenge of being Anglican chaplain at the University of the West Indies, Mona, Jamaica
- The challenge of accepting the post of vice-president in the ecumenical setting of the United Theological College of the West Indies, Jamaica
- The challenge of accepting in 1971 the principalship of the historic seminary, Codrington College, sited in Barbados
- The challenge of the post of warden/student counsellor at the University of the West Indies, Cave Hill, Barbados, 1982–1989
- The challenge of accepting in 1989 the pioneering principalship of the Simon of Cyrene Theological Institute, Wandsworth, South London, United Kingdom
- The challenge of accepting in 1994 the post of Bishop of the Windward Islands

As a teacher and preacher, Bishop Goodridge was concerned to promote the principle of equality of opportunity. Over the years, Goodridge was invited to deliver a number of notable sermons. In many of them he deployed his skills of analysis and exposition. He certainly made his congregations think. Some of his famous sermons have been collected in chapter 10 of the book, *By Divine Permission* (pp. 143–192). Attention may be drawn to the following:

- 1976 – Sermon at Westminster Abbey to mark the tenth anniversary of the independence of Barbados
- 1992 – The Mulligan Sermon preached at Gray's Inn
- 1994 – First Sermon preached as a chaplain to the Queen in the Chapel Royal, St. James's Palace
- 1995 – The Ramsden Sermon preached before the University at Great St. Mary's, the University Church, Cambridge

In summary, he issued a ringing challenge to all:

> As disciples, and as a Church, we need to hear the cries of the alienated, the exploited, the disabled and the deprived. The realities of such persons must enter the way in which we enquire and analyse, and search further truth. . . .

In our own language, from the perspective of our own culture, we hear the Word of God. The Babel of confusion is transformed by the Pentecost of communication. In our world that has shrunk by satellite communication and jet travel – two days ago I was in Barbados, now I am here in Cambridge – in a world in which boundaries are crossed so easily, the Church has a responsibility to be an international interpretative agency, helping people to meet, helping people to appreciate their differences, to recognise them and to respect them. For the Church is not a lifestyle enclave, but a community; and essential to any community is recognition of differences. The others must not be named and understood by long established territories; the others are persons, persons from different cultures, but persons nevertheless. These dry bones do live, and persons have become members of the household of God.

When he accepted the post of Anglican chaplain to the students at Mona, Jamaica in 1966, the decolonisation movement was in full flow. The Mona campus was at the centre of the maelstrom.

Goodridge was particularly attracted to the ecumenical initiatives within the region. Interestingly, adjacent to the University of the West Indies campus, there had been established an institution, the United Theological College of the West Indies. This was sponsored by eight denominations – Anglican, Methodist, Baptist, Lutheran, Church of God, Nazarene, Brethren, and Pilgrim Holiness. In 1970 Goodridge accepted the challenge of the post of deputy president of the United Theological College of the West Indies.

Goodridge's stay at the United Theological College of the West Indies was brief, and for a special reason. The Anglican Archbishop of the West Indies, the Right Reverend Alan John Knight, summoned Goodridge to answer a pre-eminent challenge – to assume the principalship of Codrington College, a venerable institution in Barbados established in the eighteenth century and linked to the Codrington Library of All Souls College, Oxford, and to Durham University. As an alumnus of the College, Goodridge was well aware of its distinctive heritage. There is general agreement that Goodridge fulfilled expectations at Codrington College. Numbers and financial circumstances were much improved.

Goodridge rose to another challenge when he shifted over to the University of the West Indies at Cave Hill, Barbados, as warden/counsellor. All were impressed by his professional mentorship skills. He was particularly well suited to the university atmosphere and rose to the challenge of teaching some courses in philosophy and ethics. With his training in history, social sciences and theology Sehon Goodridge was able to fill a niche in the unfolding panorama of the Black Atlantic in the period of the last quarter of the twentieth century to his comparatively early death in 2007. The modern West Indies was already evolving.

Meanwhile, as an increasing number of Black and minority ethnic immigrants made their way to England during the years after the end of World War II in 1945, some towns and cities became noticeably multi-racial, multi-ethnic, multi-cultural and multi-faith. The end of World War II in 1945 and a demand for labour in England created a significant movement of Afro-Caribbean migrants, sometimes dated from the arrival in Britain in 1948 of the ship *Windrush*. From that time, a West Indian community developed, especially in areas of London, Birmingham, Manchester, Liverpool and other cities.

Racial prejudice and discrimination dismayed the new arrivals. They were joined by persons from countries which had been parts of the British Empire, transformed into the Commonwealth through the process of decolonisation. Many scholars point out that only a cold reception greeted Afro-Caribbean and other migrants in Anglican and other churches.

An English bishop remarked, 'My prayer for Black Anglicans is that you may inject some of your liveliness and joyfulness in the whole body of the Church. It is one of the gifts you bring – and don't be put off if it is not at first welcomed.' His comment brings to mind a story reported concerning a Jamaican lady, newly arrived in London. After attending an Anglican service with a predominately white congregation, she complained, 'I didn't know that one could worship God so quietly.'

Adjustments had to be made on all sides.

To meet the challenge, the Church of England set up countervailing machinery. One institution was the Race, Pluralism and Community Group of the Board for Social Responsibility. Race Relations Field Officers were appointed throughout Britain.

The Synods and governing committees of the Church of England were urged to let Blacks, Asians and other minority ethnic groups take their rightful place. Their actions were to go beyond mere tokenism and paternalism. The most convenient analysis is Glynne Gordon-Carter's *An Amaz-*

*ing Journey: The Church of England's Response to Institutional Racism* (CMEAC–CHP, 2003).

The linchpin of the anti-racist thrust was the Simon of Cyrene Theological Institute. It is striking that Goodridge was selected to be the pioneering principal. It is even more remarkable that he accepted the challenge of launching this untried venture. He hit upon the name Simon of Cyrene Theological Institute with reference to the Black who had helped Christ bear the cross of Calvary on the first Good Friday. Racism awareness training was central.

As an educator, Goodridge used his skills of communication widely, attending meetings and seminars throughout the United Kingdom. One student commented that 'his scholarship challenged the intellectual potential of his students, and imbued them with the confidence to overcome their reticence and to be awake to the potential and the responsibilities of the Black community'. Far from seeking theological agreement he encouraged theological honesty.

On 6 July 1992 a report produced by the Community and Race Relations Unit of the Council of Churches for Britain and Ireland was launched at the Simon of Cyrene Theological Institute. The focus was Theological Training and Racial Justice. With a healthy dose of sarcasm, Goodridge quipped that 'after all, . . . it has been long established by David Hume that no serious thought or culture could come from Black people!' But, in the new setting, Goodridge urged that it could no longer be maintained that theology was the preserve of the middle-class White male.

England became a social laboratory where many experiments were tried in an effort to deal with the new elements in the society. Lessons could be learnt from the programmes of Coleridge and Mitchinson. Goodridge was a central figure in the intellectual and practical work required.

Recommended by the 1988 Lambeth Conference and endorsed by the Church of England General Synod in 1989, a campaign was launched, known as the Decade of Evangelism. The coordinating agency was the Church of England General Synod Board of Mission. The highlight of the Decade of Evangelism with a focus on anti-racism was the Black Anglican Celebration for the Decade, held over a never-to-be forgotten weekend at the University of York (22–24 July 1994). It was designed to affirm Black Anglicans.

As Black and minority ethnic Anglicans were beginning to make headway, it was fitting that Goodridge should be elected as Bishop of the Windward Islands in 1994. The wheel had come full circle. Goodridge's creole heritage made him eminently suited to inherit a West Indian diocese which included a section of the diocese of the first bishop, William Hart Coleridge.

In addition to his responsibilities as bishop, Goodridge continued his work at other levels. Internationally, significant advances were being made in the field of Human Rights. For example, at the 1998 Lambeth Conference, the Anglican Church was challenged to make new strides for human rights. The resolutions had been drafted by bishops working in Section One's subsection on Human Rights and Human Dignity chaired by Bishop Goodridge.

Similarly, Bishop Goodridge did not hesitate to accept the challenge to be a member of the Grenada Truth and Reconciliation Commission. He had before him the example of his fellow King's College London alumnus Archbishop Desmond Tutu of South Africa. The slogan 'Redeeming the Past: A Time for Healing' seems to owe something to Bishop Goodridge's pattern of thought. It is noteworthy that he stuck to his task despite illness and retirement in 2005. The chairman of the commission, the Honourable Donald Trotman, submitted the report to the governor general of Grenada on 28 March 2006.

There is no doubt that Bishop Goodridge was an outstanding leader within the Anglican Church and the wider community of human rights intellectuals. One indication of the esteem with which he was held was his appointment in 1993 as Royal Chaplain – an honorary chaplain to Queen Elizabeth II.

He incorporated elements of liberation theology, Black theology, feminist theology and other strands of late-twentieth-century thought into his analysis and exposition. He was able to tease out from the past lessons for the present and future.

Bishop Goodridge has surely left a lasting legacy.

Rest in peace.

## NOTE

1. A comprehensive listing of Goodridge's publications is provided in the magnificent biography by Janet Goodridge, *By Divine Permission: A Biography of the Rt. Rev. Sehon Goodridge, Bishop of the Windward Islands* (Bridgetown: Barbados Museum and Historical Society, 2011), 195–99. The listing is subdivided into books, monographs, articles, book reviews and journals. Unattributed material in the text of this foreword is drawn mainly from *By Divine Permission*.

# PREFACE TO THE FIRST EDITION

THIS BOOK IS NOT INTENDED as a biography of William Hart Coleridge, nor is it an attempt to deal specifically with the history of Barbados during the early nineteenth century. Rather, it seeks to explain why the See of Barbados and the Leeward Islands was created and how the nature of the first Bishop's appointment influenced his episcopate. The main contention is that when the British Government turned to the Established Church for assistance in the amelioration of the condition of the enslaved population in the West Indian colonies, this led to the creation of the two new Sees of Jamaica and of Barbados and the Leeward Islands in 1824, and to the appointment of two Bishops (the other being Christopher Lipscomb). We shall see how Bishop Coleridge held amelioration to be an integral part of evangelisation throughout his episcopate, from 1824 to 1842.

This book concentrates mainly on his episcopate in the island of Barbados, which had been colonised in 1627 by the English. A Colonial Church was established to serve the early settlers. For many decades it was under the jurisdiction of the Bishop of London. Chapters 1 and 2 deal with the Colonial Church before Coleridge, the circumstances of his appointment as the first Bishop of the newly created See, his role, and the special question of his jurisdiction.

Bishop Coleridge found eleven Parish Churches and four Chapels in the eleven parishes of the island. Chapter 3 shows how he increased accommodation for worshippers in town and country by providing Chapels of Ease and Chapel Schools. This involved him in a considerable building programme.

Chapter 4 shows how the Bishop set up the administrative machinery in his Diocese, recruited clergy and provided for local training by re-organising

Codrington College. The clergy in Barbados increased from 15 to 29 during his episcopate.

Bishop Coleridge considered public education integral to amelioration and evangelisation. Chapter 5 describes his great work in education, especially among the labouring class, both Black and White.

In Chapter 6 we see how the Bishop guided the pastoral care of the Church, particularly in the direction of the amelioration of the status of the enslaved population. He considered the customs of the Blacks such as Sabbath breaking, the cult of obeah, polygamy and concubinage a tremendous challenge to the Church's ministry.

The Bishop's involvement in the great social work of emancipation and apprenticeship, and his promotion of certain social institutions to help the emancipated Blacks live in society as free citizens, are described in Chapter 7.

The concluding Chapter 8 recounts the Bishop's departure from the island and his Diocese, as a result of failing health, the way in which the Diocese was administered during his absence, and the division of the Diocese into three Sees on his resignation in 1842. His continued concern for the mission of the Church of England in the British colonies is evident in his sermons at the consecrations of the Bishops of New Zealand, Tasmania and Gibraltar and of his own successors, Thomas Parry (Barbados), Daniel Gateward Davis (Antigua) and William Piercy Austin (British Guiana). Bishop Coleridge preserved the same sense of mission in his heart when he served as the first Warden of the missionary college, St. Augustine's, Canterbury, from 1848 until his death on 21 December 1849.

I hope that this book will make a contribution towards the material for studying the origins and development of the Church in the Caribbean. It of course deals only with a small period of the history of one Church. It was a period that was crucial for both Church and society; and the quality of the man who directed that Church's conduct and the magnitude of his labours and their achievements cast a flood of beneficial light on that dark period, which can still illuminate present pathways.

This book is intended to be of interest to the general reader, but I hope that it will also prove useful to students in our schools, colleges, and University. I have accordingly been punctilious in providing references – especially to the large number of unpublished sources which I have been privileged to examine. In this connection I wish to express my sincere thanks to the owners and custodians of these materials both for permitting access to them and for allowing me to publish extracts from them in my book.

I must also thank the Board of Governors of Codrington College for granting me sabbatical leave for the academic year 1979–80, and the Director and Committee of the Programme on Theological Education (PTE) of the World Council of Churches (WCC) and the United Society for the Propagation of the Gospel (USPG) for their generous grants towards this leave. This year has afforded me a wonderful opportunity for research, reflection and writing.

I am also indebted to the Governing Body of Wolfson College and to the Warden and Fellows of All Souls College, Oxford, for electing me respectively a member of the Common Room of their colleges for the year. I am also grateful to the Governing Body of The Queen's College, Oxford, for appointing me to act as Chaplain during the Michaelmas Term while the chaplain, the Rev. Anthony Harvey (1980 Bampton Lecturer), was on leave, and Assistant Chaplain for the rest of the year. The community of Queen's has been a great source of inspiration to me.

I am indeed indebted to many others, but permit me to mention Dr. Keith Hunte, Senior Lecturer in the Department of History, University of the West Indies, who read the draft chapters and made most valuable comments on them. I must also mention Mr. John Simmons, Librarian of All Souls College, Oxford, who read the draft manuscript and offered some most useful comments. That the text is before us is due in large measure to Miss Patricia Lloyd, Fellows' Secretary, The Queen's College, Oxford, who patiently typed the final drafts. To her I am extremely grateful.

Finally, I thank the Secretary and Committee of the Missions Department, the SPCK, for a generous grant towards the publication of my work by the CEDAR Press.

SEHON GOODRIDGE
Principal
Codrington College
Barbados
October 1980

# 1

# THE COLONIAL CHURCH BEFORE 1824

ACCORDING TO C.F. PASCOE, the Society for the Propagation of the Gospel in Foreign Parts sought as early as 1715 (or 1713, the dates are conflicting) to establish two Bishoprics in the West Indies, but the Society's efforts were not crowned with success until 1824 when two new Sees were constituted in Jamaica and Barbados respectively, the latter to receive William Coleridge as Bishop.[1] The work of the Society, and indeed of the Church of England as a whole, in the West Indian colonies was impeded by the lack of proper order and episcopal oversight. According to one judgement, the Church in the West Indies between 1600 and 1800 was an 'anomaly', an episcopal Church without bishops.[2] The failure to provide for an episcopate in the colonies was due, in W.W. Manross's view, not only to the lack of persistent interest in the colonies on the part of the English government during the eighteenth century, but also to the unwillingness of the government to interfere in the religious and political affairs in the colonies, lest the results proved unsettling. In the colonies where the majority were members of the Church of England, the provincial assemblies made provision for the maintenance of the Church, though not always on terms acceptable to the authorities in England.[3]

In all the English colonies, except Rhode Island and Connecticut, Governors were appointed by the King, or by proprietors. Most colonies had Legislative Councils with powers to appoint, and all had elected Assemblies. Governors became leaders of the Church in the colonies, performing such ecclesiastical duties as granting licences to marry and probating of wills. In colonies where the Church was established the Governor was regarded as 'Ordinary', with powers to investigate the qualifications of newly arrived ministers and induct them to parishes either upon presentation by vestries or upon his own initiative. The Governor could also deprive unworthy clergymen of their benefices and, in some cases, suspend or depose them from their ministry. The assumption of this power to deprive, suspend and depose was generally opposed by ecclesiastical authorities in England and by commissaries in the colonies, as being inconsistent with the constitution of the Church of England. There were no ecclesiastical courts in the colonies, and the Governor tended to promote the interest of the authority that appointed him, be it royal or proprietary.[4] In Barbados, as in Jamaica and elsewhere in the colonies, the clergy and ecclesiastical affairs were under the jurisdiction of the Bishop of London. The origin of this jurisdiction is obscure; no conscious formal arrangement can be traced. It has been suggested that the request from the Virginia Company to Bishop King in 1620 that ministers be provided for that colony, probably set one precedent, and that the jurisdiction over English trading-ports in the Netherlands, which Archbishop Laud obtained for the See of London in 1633, probably set another precedent.

In 1675 the Lords Committee of Trade and Plantations, at the request of Bishop Compton, directed that an inquiry be made concerning this matter of jurisdiction. In 1685 the Committee approved the jurisdiction of the Bishop of London over the West Indian colonies, with the exception that the powers of disposal of parishes, licensing of marriages and probating of wills be reserved to Governors.[6] Bishop Compton adapted the policy of delegating authority in the colonies to resident clergy, specially commissioned and given the title of 'commissaries'. These were usually incumbents of the chief benefices in the colonies and, depending upon their personal character and the circumstances, holders of much authority. Where the Church was not established their office was honorary. Their duties were to preside over voluntary meetings of clergy and to correspond with the Bishop. In colonies where the Church was established commissaries assumed power to summon meetings of the clergy and preside over them ('visitations'); seized the opportunity to rebuke the clergy for any misdemeanours, and claimed the right to suspend negligent or immoral ministers after due trial. The authority of commissaries was indefinite, so clergy – and sometimes Governors – resisted it.[7]

Enquiries concerning the nature of the Bishop of London's jurisdiction over the Church in the colonies were again made by Bishop Edmund Gibson, who came to the See in 1723. He was unhappy about the basis of his authority, and appealed to the Privy Council for a definite ruling. The Attorney General and Solicitor General ruled that the ecclesiastical jurisdiction of the colonies remained with the Crown, and that the Bishop of London had to obtain a royal commission in order to exercise his authority abroad. Gibson agreed and his authority was given formal legality, much to the satisfaction of commissaries whose hands were thereby strengthened. Gibson's successor, Bishop Thomas Sherlock, anxious to please the authorities, did not appoint new commissaries to replace those who had died or retired, and he took care not to infringe the royal prerogative. His successors' position was even more tenuous than his predecessors', consisting mainly in granting the required certificates of episcopal ordination to ministers going to the colonies.[8]

Let us look more specifically at the Bishop of London's jurisdiction in Barbados through the appointment of commissaries. On 13 May 1690 Colonel James Kendall, Governor of Barbados, informed the Board (i.e. the Council) that the Bishop of London had appointed the Rev. Mr. William Walker commissary in matters ecclesiastical, though the origin of the authority of the Bishop as Ordinary of all English colonies in the Americas was uncertain, according to the opinion of the then Lords of Trade.[9] Mr. Walker was Rector of All Saints in the Parish of St. Peter. As Commissary or Surrogate (or Vice-Bishop) he would have power to create 'Spiritual Courts' and exercise ecclesiastical jurisdiction over the laity, the Bishop reserving jurisdiction over the clergy, who were ordained by him and sent out with letters to the Governor. The Governor, as the King's deputy, exercised the authority of Ordinary with responsibility for issuing marriage licences and probates of wills, and, as patron of parishes presenting and collating clergy to benefices, of which he could also deprive them on petition from parishioners.[10] The Bishop of London on one occasion directed Governor Lowther not to interfere with his commissary, Gordon, and not to collate to livings any persons but those introduced and recommended to him by himself *qua* Bishop of London.[11] The Bishop also reserved to himself and his commissary the right to grant leave of absence to the clergy, as in the case of the Rev. Dr. Charles Irvine, 8 June 1721.[12]

Various commissaries were appointed by the Bishop of London, but they were not restricted to particular parishes. No record of commissaries can be found in the Vestry Books of St. Michael after 1742.[13] Commissaries ranged in character and acceptance from the 'pious and learned' Cryer to the flamboyant and controversial William Gordon. It was felt that the appointment of the latter as commissary brought great discredit to the clerical profession. As one who had risen from the status of an indentured servant to the status of a clergyman and who was reputed to be intent on fortune through fraud, smuggling and perjury, he became to the aristocracy and to Governor Lowther an object of contempt. He was considered to be a 'factious, low-bred and intermedling clergyman' and Governor Lowther, incensed by hatred of him, questioned the authority of the Bishop of London and put an end to the 'Spiritual Courts', which were considered a threat to the civil government and municipal laws.[14] The clamour and disquietude of the inhabitants of the island and the intense hatred of Gordon gave Lowther his chance. He enacted that no Ecclesiastical Law or Jurisdiction should have power to enforce, confirm, or establish any 'mulct' or punishment in any case in the island, and that all sentences and judgements of 'Spiritual Courts' should be declared null and void.[15]

Successive Bishops of London wanted to be relieved of the mere appearance of authority over ecclesiastical affairs in the West Indian colonies and to press for the constitution of Sees, but they were up against the fear in the minds of members of the ruling class that the establishment of an episcopate locally would have serious consequences, insofar as it would set up an authority to rival theirs. There was also the question of financial provision. Who would bear the cost of the episcopate, the local taxpayers or the British Treasury?

These factors must be set within the context of the great debate between the abolitionists and the slave-owning interests with regard to slavery in the West Indian colonies. This debate began towards the end of the eighteenth century and continued until 1823, when the British Parliament through the Canning Resolutions committed itself to the ultimate emancipation of the enslaved people and urged proprietors to gear themselves for this eventuality. A brief reference to this debate, and its outcome, will help us to determine the immediate factors that led to the constitution of dioceses in the West Indian colonies, of which Barbados was one.

From the start, mention must be made of the untiring efforts of Bishop Beilby Porteus (Bishop of Chester and, later, of London) to give life to the moribund members of the Church in the colonies at the turn of the eighteenth century. He urged the religious instruction of Blacks, and in 1794 the Society for the Conversion and Religious Instruction and Education of the Negro Slaves in the British West Indian Islands, which had its genesis in the bequest of the Hon. Robert Boyle in 1691, received its first Royal Charter through his exertions.[16] Bishop Porteus also sent university-trained clergymen to the West Indies. 'Amelioration' was the watchword which the planters in the colonies opposed to 'abolition', the war-cry of the humanitarians in England and of the Dissenters in the colonies.

The Abolitionists, fired by the enthusiasm of William Fox, supported by William Wilberforce and backed by Lord Grenville, won the day for the abolition of the slave trade in 1807. The abolitionists continued to attack the institution of slavery on the grounds of long hours of labour, inadequate clothing and food, and the inhumane discipline of the enslaved workers. The great charge was that enslavement was incompatible with the Christianisation of Blacks. In the West Indies the Dissenters were asserting their right to be in society and to preach the gospel without molestation, thus incurring the wrath of planters. In Barbados there was a riot against the Dissenters and the Wesleyan Chapel in Bridgetown was burnt down in 1823.[17] The witness of the Dissenters and Sectarian missionaries has been extolled by L.J. Ragatz, who also states categorically that the role of the Established Church in Caribbean missionary activities was negligible.[18]

There is no gainsaying the tremendous witness of the Dissenters, but the work of the Established Church in Barbados mainly through the work of the Society for the Propagation of the Gospel in Foreign Parts (SPG, now USPG) on the Codrington Estates[19] cannot be overlooked. By providing better housing with garden spaces, two hospitals for better medical care, more adequate clothing and food, largely through the right to own money by reducing the hours of labour on the estates, and especially those of the young, allowing them to receive instruction; by establishing a chaplain in the person of the Rev. John Hothersall Pinder who encouraged marriages, instituted Sunday Schools, adopted the school system of Andrew Bell and administered the Lord's Supper – by all these measures the Society's work in ameliorating the conditions of the enslaved workers on the Codrington estates is worthy of commendation.[20] With the arrival of the first Bishop of Barbados the Society felt confident that their policy for the enslaved workers on these estates would be put into effect.[21]

In fact, it was to the Church that the British government looked for guaranteeing the implementation of the policy of Amelioration, and this led to the establishing of the two Sees of Barbados and Jamaica. Given the lack of proper episcopal jurisdiction in the colonies it was essential that this be rectified if the Church was to play the vital role of helping to implement the Canning Resolutions set out in the Bathurst Dispatches of 1823; religious instruction to be offered to enslaved people, Parliament making provision for an adequate number of clergy and teachers under episcopal oversight, Sunday markets to be abolished; laws to be passed enabling an enslaved person to give testimony if he could produce a certificate from a religious instructor to show that he understood the nature of an oath; marriage to be encouraged, and mothers with a number of legitimate children to be exempt from field-labour; restrictions on manumissions to be enforced, and control to be placed on punishment, with proper records kept of whippings in excess of three lashes; savings banks to be established to enable enslaved persons to save and purchase their freedom.[22]

The British Parliament had obviously committed itself to a policy of amelioration which would lead to emancipation. There is small wonder that the various colonial legislatures resisted the proposed reforms. In Barbados the Council refused to adopt them. In the face of uproar, riots and the violence meted out to missionaries, Canning turned to the Established Church. He announced that the government had decided to strengthen the Church in the West Indies by establishing two Dioceses, and that the British Exchequer would provide for their administrative expenses. Thus in the year 1824 were born the Dioceses of Barbados and Jamaica.[23]

# 2

## First Bishop
### His Role and Jurisdiction

WILLIAM HART COLERIDGE WAS born in 1789, the only son of Luke Herman Coleridge of Thorverton, Devonshire, by his wife, the third daughter of Richard Hart of Exeter. His father, brother of the famous poet, Samuel Taylor Coleridge, died while William Hart Coleridge was an infant. So he was educated by his uncle, the Rev. George Coleridge, master of the Grammar School of Ottery St. Mary.[1] He matriculated at Christ Church, Oxford, as a Commoner in January 1808 at the age of 18.[2] On 21 November 1811 he graduated with the BA, and on 1 June 1814 he obtained the MA.[3]

We are also told that he obtained two Firsts, one in Classics and one in Mathematics.[4] At the time of his nomination to the newly created Bishopric of Barbados, he was granted the BD and DD of Oxford on 17 and 18 June 1824 respectively.[5] After leaving Oxford, he became one of the curates of St. Andrew's, Holborn, where, incidentally, the young Benjamin Disraeli, future British Prime Minister, was baptised on 31 July 1817. After serving his curacy he was appointed Secretary to the Society for Promoting Christian Knowledge (SPCK), from which post he was appointed and consecrated first Bishop of Barbados and the Leeward Islands in 1824.[6]

Early in that year, Coleridge had been identified as a suitable person for appointment as Bishop of one of the two dioceses. On 23 January 1824 the Bishop of London wrote to him with the news that His Majesty's Government had considered establishing two Bishoprics in the West Indies with the conviction that religious instruction for the amelioration of the condition of the enslaved population would be advanced if put under episcopal oversight. The Bishop also mentioned that much depended on the character and conduct of the persons chosen, so Coleridge was being consulted as one of those whose professional connections were best suited to assist in the selection, for he had shown much enthusiasm as curate of St. Andrew's, Holborn. The Bishop further informed Coleridge that he would submit his name to His Majesty, if he were willing to accept the appointment of Bishop of the 'Leeward Islands', and that the sum of £4,000 sterling per annum would be 'annexed to the Bishopric' with the guarantee that after twelve years, on retirement, he would be entitled to a pension of £1,000.[7]

This is a clear indication of the high esteem in which Coleridge was held by his ecclesiastical superiors and the role they envisaged he would play as first Bishop of Barbados. He was appointed and consecrated at Lambeth on 25 July 1824. Also, for the Diocese of Jamaica the Rev. Christopher Lipscomb, DD, was appointed and consecrated Bishop. C.F. Pascoe records the immense pleasure that this event gave SPG who felt that they had achieved the goal for which they had striven from very early in the eighteenth century.[8]

The Letters Patent establishing the See of Barbados gave the Bishop the same general ecclesiastical jurisdiction in the diocese as English bishops had in theirs, except that the nature of this jurisdiction vis-à-vis the authority of the Governor as Ordinary had yet to be settled. After alluding to the difficulty of supplying ordained clergy for the colonies and the lack of pastoral oversight and care which the people were experiencing, the Letters Patent went on to constitute the islands[9] of Barbados, Grenada, Saint Vincent, Dominica, Antigua and Montserrat, Saint Christopher, Nevis, the Virgin Islands, Trinidad, Tobago and Saint Lucia, and 'their respective dependencies', the 'Bishopric of Barbados and the Leeward Islands', 'we having great confidence in the learning, morals, probity and prudence of our well beloved William Hart Coleridge, Doctor in Divinity, do name and appoint him to be a Bishop of the said See, so that he the said William Hart Coleridge shall be taken to be the Bishop of the Bishop's See',[10] which would be within the Province of Canterbury.

There are some other provisions which highlight the great significance

Coleridge's appointment had for the British government. On 5 November 1824 Doctors Commons gave their judgement that an Englishman with a degree from Oxford and ordained by the Bishop of Barbados, could hold preferment on his return to England, and also that a native of Barbados, ordained by the Bishop of Barbados, could hold preferment in England.[11] On 16 November 1824 J.W. Horton, on the instructions of Lord Bathurst, Secretary of State for the Colonies, wrote to Coleridge, informing him that he could constitute archdeaconries in the same way as hitherto obtained in colonial Sees, and that Letters Patent would be issued by His Majesty, enabling him to constitute and collate such archdeaconries as he selected, subject to recommendation by the Secretary of State and approval by the King, who reserved the right to cancel any appointment. Coleridge was also informed that the King was pleased with the recommendation that the Rev. Mr. Parry be appointed archdeacon of Antigua.[12]

The exceptionally generous financial arrangements for the new Bishop and the provisions for his conveyance to Barbados also demonstrate the political significance of his appointment. As mentioned above, he was guaranteed £4,000 sterling a year. Caldecott, however, states that the British Exchequer committed itself to £5,500 sterling a year for the Bishop, £2,800 for an archdeacon, and £2,500 for six curates.[13] A letter to the Bishop of London from Lord Liverpool, dated 21 June 1824, shows the care that was taken to make adequate arrangements for the new West Indian Bishops: their salaries would be paid from 'Lady Day last' to cover some of the expenses of their 'outfit'; houses would be provided for them and kept in good repair at 'Public Expense'; in collaboration with the Board of Admiralty arrangements would be made for the 'Conveyance of the Bishops to the Islands under their Jurisdiction', and the Captain would be properly remunerated for the 'Expenses of his Table' during the conveyance.[14]

The pomp and ceremony on the arrival and introduction of Bishop Coleridge to his See in January 1825 was charged with political as well as ecclesiastical significance. The *Barbadian* was happy to announce the arrival of HMS *Herald* with the 'long and anxiously expected Bishops of Jamaica and Barbados'. Amidst the general expectation in the island the ship was indeed 'Herald of much good to the Colonies'. The *Barbadian* went on: 'Sure we are that the Right Reverend Gentlemen, who have been selected from the very numerous and enlightened body of the English

Clergy to superintend the Ecclesiastical Establishment of the West Indian Colonies, will be received with a feeling corresponding with the gracious intention of our Sovereign.' The *Barbadian* further gave the list of passengers on board HMS *Herald*: the Right Rev. Christopher Lipscomb, DD, Lord Bishop of Jamaica, his lady, and the Honourable Mr. Coventry; Rev. Mr. Pope, Archdeacon of Jamaica; Mr. Lipscomb, secretary to Bishop Lipscomb; the Right Rev. William Hart Coleridge, DD, Lord Bishop of Barbados, and Mr. Coleridge, his Lordship's secretary; the Rev. Mr. Parry, Archdeacon of Antigua and his lady, Rev. Mr. Adam, Rev. Mr. Goddard and lady, Rev. Mr. Paterson and Rev. Mr. Bolton.[15] Bishop Lipscomb and his party arrived in Jamaica in February. It is obvious that care was taken to have administrative assistance within the family circles, trusted archdeacons and a nucleus of dependable clergy.

When the *Herald* anchored at the upper steps of the wharf in Bridgetown, Bishop Coleridge was waited on by two aides-de-camp from the Governor and by a deputation from the clergy. Arrangements had been made for his landing on 29th January, the anniversary of His Majesty's Accession. On that day, therefore, he took the salute from the ship in the harbour and, accompanied by the Captain who had taken such good care of him, he went ashore. He was received by a Guard of Honour of the 35th Regiment, in attendance by command of the Governor, forming a line on each side from Trafalgar Square to St. Michael's Church to which he was conducted by the clergy amidst joy 'from all classes of persons'. The Rector, the Rev. Mr. Garnett, conducted the Bishop to the Chair prepared for him, and the Bishop's secretary read aloud the Royal Commission and the Certificate of his Consecration. The Bishop was then ushered to his Stall and presided over the Communion Service. The church, packed to capacity, was full of excitement and happiness, as everyone was delighted to have 'our own bishop', was charmed by his voice and manner of reading the Commandments and the Prayers for the Service, and was in rapt silence as he pronounced the blessing.[16]

The *Barbadian* further depicts the Establishment spirit that prevailed:

> They only who have been nurtured in loyalty, who have imbibed monarchical principles, who have been taught to appreciate justly the blessings of the British Constitution, and who fondly cling, even amidst the alarming symp-

toms of decline, and the incessant attacks of her open and insidious enemies, to the beautiful and incomparable form of our Established Church, can conceive the nature of the emotions which the impressive scene of Saturday called forth ... the 29th of January, 1825, will, indeed, be a memorable era in the history of our country.[17]

On the same day as the Bishop's installation, he and the Honourable James Holder Alleyne were sworn in as members of the Board of Council.[18] To conclude the events of the introduction of the Bishop to his See, the clergy visited him at his residence, 'Gibraltar', and the Senior Rector, the Rev. Mr. Garnett, read an address congratulating him on his appointment and arrival, to which he graciously and lucidly replied.[19]

The choice of the Bishop's residence, 'Gibraltar', and the provisions for its furnishing and maintenance, indicate the strategic position of the Bishop in relation to the centres of political power. Bishop Coleridge himself stated that on his arrival he found 'Gibraltar' completely furnished, and that it was situated 'on an eminence', 'at a convenient distance from the Town, Government House and the Garrison'. He further mentioned that with some additions 'Gibraltar' would be a respectable residence for him; he had paid the interest on the purchase money – which was £6,000 sterling – and he would like authorisation to conclude the purchase of the house and make such additions as he thought necessary.[20] In setting out his request formally he begged leave to purchase 'Gibraltar' for his residence, with a grant for repairs and additions of library, sitting-room, Chaplain's room and Chapel, and also for more stables and offices. He also requested permission to purchase the Pine Estate to enlarge the Bishop's grounds; the Black dwellings of which estate would be removed to 'a more distant spot' in order to provide a residence for the Archdeacon. As he saw it, all the grounds between Government House and 'Bishop's Palace' would be 'uninterrupted', in the hands of the government, and the Archdeacon would always be near both the Bishop and the Governor. The whole purchase and improvement of 'Gibraltar' and the Pine, and grounds, was estimated at £15,000 sterling.[21] It is evident that the Bishop himself had no illusion about the significance of his position in relation to the centre of political power in the island.

From the outset, Bishop Coleridge was concerned about the nature of his jurisdiction as the first colonial Bishop in Barbados. Very early he set out his thoughts on this matter. First, he expressed his view that the clergy should be more independent, and he recommended that their salaries be paid out of the Treasury and not from the vestries of their respective parishes. He also advocated that the salary for the clergy be raised from £300 currency to £500. Secondly, he considered that he should be constituted ecclesiastical guardian of churches, burial grounds, parsonage houses, school houses and so on, with power to initiate the necessary repairs. This would further take out of the hands of the vestries the power they had over the clergy. Thirdly, he considered that the Bishop should be made 'full Ordinary', wresting from the hands of the Governor the power to collate to livings, and grant licences and probates of wills. Fourthly, he urged that all ecclesiastical patronage which was promised to him should be transferred to him in order that both 'censure and reward' be in the same hands. Fifthly, he argued that Ecclesiastical Law in the islands should enable the Bishop to place the vestries on a better footing, and that the application of the Ecclesiastical Law of England would constitute the Bishop 'full Ordinary' and 'Sole Patron' in the 'distant Diocese'.[22] He further requested that the power of his Patent be fully defined, since he was, in the opinion of the Solicitor General, 'full Ordinary' of Antigua. Finally, he informed both the SPG and the Society for the Conversion of Blacks that their respective Chaplains should obtain licences from him.[23]

The first response from the British government concerning this matter of jurisdiction came on 30 June 1825 when Earl Bathurst sent a circular to all Colonial Governors in the West Indies, instructing them that, in the event of any benefices falling vacant they should inform either the Bishop of Barbados and the Leeward Islands or the Bishop of Jamaica, to discover whether he had any clergyman to fill the vacancy. If the Bishop had a clergyman, then the respective Governor could proceed to collate him to the vacant benefice. If the Bishop had no clergyman, then the matter should be reported to His Majesty who, on the advice of the Archbishop of Canterbury and the Board of Right Reverend and Reverend Members recently appointed for this purpose, would nominate some clergyman for the vacant benefice.[24] It is clear that in the eyes of the British government the Colonial Governor still had the power to collate. The question, therefore, was whether this would be changed, now that there was a Colonial Bishop.

Bishop Coleridge put the challenge squarely. He requested a judgement as to whether, given his Patent of Appointment, collation to benefices, granting of marriage licences, probates of wills and letters of administration should continue in the hands of the Governor or should be rescinded with the appointment of the new Bishop. He wanted a clear definition of duties of Bishop and Governor in collating and granting institutions to benefices. On 16 July 1825 Doctors Commons replied that, in the opinion of the Crown Lawyers, the appointment of the Bishop had made no difference to the previous power of the Governor to grant marriage licences, probates and administrations; that the Governor was to collate 'as in England' in the case of free Chapels, while the Bishop was to grant Institution which might apply to patronage of private 'individuals'; that the original terms of the Bishop's appointment expressed the intention that he should collate, and so it was probably fitting to alter previous instructions to the Governor and to direct him 'to present to the Bishop for Institution'.

The British government was obviously in a dilemma, for it was clear that by the nature of his appointment the Bishop was on firm ground, and yet there would be much embarrassment if the powers of the Colonial Governor were revoked. There is little surprise, then, that the British government wrote to Bishop Coleridge on 10 January 1826, informing him that he might have misunderstood the Crown Lawyers' judgement and that he should follow the confidential letter which he had received from Earl Bathurst, dated 9 July 1825, in which it had been stated that in colonies where Governors were appointed before a Bishop, the Bishop should consult with them concerning the filling of vacant benefices, the Governors having the right to recommend to the Bishop for Institution.[25] The whole issue had become very complicated by this stage.

It was not until 29 June 1829 that the British government sent a circular to the Governors, informing them that instead of collating to benefices, as they had been directed by the letter of Bathurst, 30 June 1825, they should present clergymen to the Bishop for Institution 'according to the form usually employed where there is Episcopal Jurisdiction'.[26] This was a definite move in the direction of full Episcopal Jurisdiction. The Bishop himself received a letter from the British government, dated 14 February 1829, informing him about the alterations made to the instructions to colonial Governors concerning ecclesiastical benefices in his diocese. The Bishop was also advised about certain guidelines for the future: the Bishop was to recommend to the Governor, to fill a vacant benefice, a person who had been officiating in the diocese for at least six months before the vacancy occurred; if the Governor objected, then he must state the grounds of his objections and notify the British government; if there was no candidate, then the Governor should notify the Secretary of State in order that a suitable person might be sent from England; if the clergyman's stipend in the benefice, which had fallen vacant, was met from Parliamentary grants, then the British government should be informed, so that arrangements could be made for his successor.[27] Clearly the duty of nominating a clergyman to a benefice, by Royal Instruction, now devolved upon the Bishop. Also, while it was evident that the Letters Patent had shown that it was the Bishop's power to collate, collation was resolved into two parts, 'Presentation' and 'Institution', thus establishing the Bishop's full jurisdiction, with no great embarrassment to the Governor.

The jurisdiction of the first Bishop of Barbados was firmly established. This was important for his position in both Church and State, charged as he was with episcopal oversight at a time when the British government saw his office as significant in advancing their policy of Amelioration among the slaves in Barbados.

# 3

# PLACES OF WORSHIP
## PARISH CHURCHES, CHAPELS AND CHAPEL SCHOOLS

BISHOP COLERIDGE WELL UNDERSTOOD that he owed his appointment to the desire of the Imperial Government to give impetus to the outreach of the Church among the slaves. He therefore considered it his first task to survey the physical resources of a Church which, prior to his appointment, had made no special effort to accommodate the underprivileged section of the Barbadian society, numbering just over 80,000 out of a population of about 100,000.

The Bishop made a tour of his entire Diocese in 1825. In Barbados he found eleven parish churches, one Chapel of Ease at All Saints in St. Peter, and Society Chapel on the Codrington Trust Estates in St. John where also was the Chapel at Codrington College, in the sole charge of the principal. He found these churches and chapels to be in better condition than he had expected, except for the one criticism that many were without fonts and none had the Ten Commandments inscribed above the altar.[1]

The accommodation in the parish churches and at All Saints' Chapel in 1825 was given as shown in table 3.1.

The above survey shows that the total seating capacity was 11,860 and the total estimated congregation was 14,585 worshippers.[2] At this time a substantial portion of this seating capacity was reserved for pew-renters, whether they attended church regularly or not. Consequently, the physical

Table 3.1

| Church | Seating Capacity | Aggregate Number of Worshippers |
| --- | --- | --- |
| St. Michael's Cathedral | 1,700 | 3,000 |
| Christ Church | 1,300 | 1,000 |
| St. Philip | 1,200 | 800 |
| St. John | 1,200 | 1,600 |
| St. Joseph | 800 | 2000 |
| St. Andrew | 750 | 700 |
| St. Lucy | 1,200 | 2,000 |
| St. Peter | 1,000 | 450 |
| St. James | 550 | 360 |
| St. Thomas | 810 | 650 |
| St. George | 900 | 1,800 |
| All Saints | 450 | 225 |

plant was evidently not adequate to meet the requirements of a growing body of worshippers. The Bishop saw that an increase in the seating capacity should be given top priority. He wasted no time. In December 1825 he wrote to Lord Bathurst describing the conditions in his Diocese and requesting assistance with the provision of four chapels and five parsonage houses.[3] Four years later he saw his first Chapels of Ease erected.

The Bishop turned his attention early to the parish of St. Michael. The Parish Church, now his Cathedral, was inadequate for a population of 20,000. He made capital of the hope, long expressed by people, of having a church erected in some other part of the town. Earlier meetings on this subject had evidently been held, but renewed impetus was given by the Bishop who summoned a meeting at the Temple, Bridge Town, on 4 May 1825, over which he presided with full support from the Governor, Sir Henry Warde, KCB. 'The Church Building Fund' was established and a Committee was appointed, comprising the Bishop, Hon. J.A. Beckles, Hon. R. Hamden, Hon. J. Brathwaite, Hon. N. Lucas, Hon. and Rev. J.H. Gittens, Hon. W. Gill, Hon. R. Haynes, Rev. W. Garnett (Rector of St.

Michael), G.M. Hinds, H.S. Cummins, G. Jemmett, J. Barrow, M. Coulthurst, J.D. Maycock, W. Oxley, W. Eversley, F. Clarke, A. King, Messrs. Higginson, Deane and Scott (Treasurers), and W. Eversley, Esq. (Secretary).[4]

The Bishop was soon able to report that a church would be erected in the Old Churchyard (previous site of the Church of St. Michael); that a subscription of £2,000 currency had already been collected; and that he had laid the first stone of 'St. Mary's Chapel' which, when completed, would accommodate 2,000. He went on to state that the new church would 'increase the respectability of that part of Town and the value of the property in that quarter'. He also declared that the church was intended for the White and Coloured population, the former occupying the body of the church, the latter the galleries.[5] The building was to be 'plain' but large and substantial, and work would begin as soon as £5,000 currency was raised. The Bishop wrote to Lord Bathurst in 1825, but had to send a 'hastener' in 1826 and was informed later that year that His Majesty's Government would contribute the £5,000 required.[6] St. Mary's was completed and consecrated in 1827, at a cost of £13,000 currency (£8,666 sterling) raised as shown in table 3.2.[7]

The Bishop disclosed his intention of introducing a bill to divide St. Michael's into two ecclesiastical parishes, St. Michael's and St. Mary's, both remaining under one Vestry for civil purposes; for example, the election of representatives to the Assembly. He also thought that the 'Pastor' of St. Mary's should be supported from pew rents, and that the maintenance of the Church should not constitute an extra burden on the Parish. For the time being, the new church would be a 'Chapel of Ease' to St. Michael's Church, and the 'Pastor' would be Curate to the Rector.[8] St. Mary's, how-

Table 3.2

| Source | Currency | Sterling |
| --- | --- | --- |
| Barbados Legislature | £5,000 | £3,333 |
| H.M. Government | £5,000 | £3,333 |
| Private Subscriptions | £3,000 | £2,000 |
| Total | 13,000 | £8,666 |

ever, was to grow and assume the character of a city church rather than that of a Chapel of Ease, and so St. Mary's is not reckoned among Bishop Coleridge's Chapels of Ease.[9]

The case of St. Mary's is important in that it shows the way in which the new Bishop faced the task of increasing the accommodation to meet the Church's more active role. He took advantage of the promise of the British government to assist in extending religion in the colonies. He astutely combined a grant from the British government with a matching grant from the local Legislature and a sum raised from local subscriptions. He saw that the pew rent system was a potential source of revenue for the maintenance of the church building and the provision of stipends for the clergy. In this regard he was doubtless over-ambitious for it was unlikely that the worshippers would have agreed to pay at a level required to meet such costs. Also, by attempting to work pew-rental into the fabric of his church-building programme he would be institutionalising the seating arrangements by classes in churches, a source of much controversy, as we shall see later.

For the Church to serve the population in various areas, particularly those in which people found it difficult to reach the parish churches, since they had no access to horse-transport, the Bishop saw the need for Chapels of Ease within the parish boundaries, and giving ease of access to some place of worship. As he saw it in 1825, a Chapel of Ease was required in Carlisle Bay, Bridge Town, on the site called Ribbitz's Ground; a chapel was needed for the windward area of St. Lucy; he noted that at St. Thomas a subscription had already been launched, and stood at the sum of £330 currency, for rebuilding a 'chapel' destroyed by the hurricane of 1780; at the Crane in St. Philip, 'a much frequented bathing resort', a chapel was needed; at Oistin in Christ Church and at Hole Town in St. James chapels should be built. He summed up the situation in this way: 'We shall have thirteen Churches and Chapels built, and open twice on every Sunday, and in some instances during the week; one Chapel of large dimensions building, two in agitation, and two more, which I doubt not of setting on foot, if Government are liberal in their aid.'[10]

The Bishop set about his building programme with generous support from His Majesty's Government, the SPG, the SPCK, the West India Building Fund, the colonial Legislature, parochial taxation and private subscriptions.¹¹ In 1829 Holy Trinity and St. Matthew were erected in the parishes of St. Philip and St. Michael respectively. In 1830 St. Luke in the parish of St. George, and in 1831 St. Paul in St. Michael, St. Bartholomew in Christ Church and St. Mark in St. John, were all built. These six Chapels of Ease provided an additional accommodation of some 3,880 for an estimated 3,535 worshippers at a total cost of £7,442 currency.¹²

The Bishop's building programme, however, suffered a disastrous setback by the devastating hurricane of 11 August 1831. The Chapels of Ease as well as seven parish churches, All Saints' Chapel and Society Chapel were destroyed. Coleridge was undaunted. He received such a generous response to his appeal for funds that the Hurricane Subscription Fund reached the handsome figure of £14,628 currency.¹³ By 1833 he had managed to reconstruct five of the Chapels of Ease, and the sixth, St. Bartholomew, was completed in 1837. The Society Chapel was rebuilt in 1833, but All Saints' Chapel was not completed until 1843. The Bishop obviously gave maximum priority to the Chapels of Ease.

With regard to the seven parish churches, St. John, St. Philip, Christ Church, St. Thomas, St. Peter, St. Lucy and St. Joseph, these lay in ruins for some time. A variety of alternative accommodation for the worshippers had to be provided. In St. John there were two chapels capable of holding 800 (St. Mark's and Society Chapel) but they were still inadequate. The parsonage was therefore licensed as a place of worship, but this could only hold 250. In St. Philip, between Holy Trinity and the licensed chapel there was accommodation for 550. In Christ Church 600 were accommodated in the Fort and St. Bartholomew. In St. Thomas 80 could assemble in the porch and part of the church. In St. Peter a licensed house was provided to hold 200. In St. Lucy the school-house was used to accommodate 230 and in St. Joseph 200 could assemble in the licensed parsonage. The devastation wrought by the hurricane had radically reduced the accommodation for worshippers. In seven parishes of a total population of about 60,000 the church accommodation was now no more than about 3,000.¹⁴

Bishop Coleridge turned his attention to the Parliamentary Grant for the relief of sufferers from the hurricane, which was administered by a General Committee of which he was Chairman. The first portion of this Grant had been received – £25,500 sterling – and was to be distributed to all who were 'indigent and necessitous'. The Proprietors also pressed for a claim on the Grant, but the Bishop contended that only after the poor and needy were provided for could distribution be made more generally.

Then came the important request to the Governor, Sir Lionel Smith. The Bishop informed him of a petition from the Commissioners that by a Resolution of the Commissioners, signed by the Governor himself, the Speaker and the Bishop, the remaining portion of the Grant be applied to assist the re-erection of the seven parish churches destroyed by the hurricane. The Bishop confessed that this measure would contravene the instructions from His Majesty's Government concerning the purpose and use of the Grant, but he argued that the Barbadian government had informed the bishops in the West Indies that there was no more money available for the erection of churches and chapels in their respective dioceses, and that the parishes could not meet the necessary expenses. It was true, the Bishop admitted, that a church could not qualify as a 'public building', but he contended that 'every soul' was concerned for the Church; the poor benefited more from the 'comforts of a well-spent Sabbath' and the observance of public worship than their 'more affluent and independent brethren'. Also, the Bishop thought that the poor man who had to provide for his family, and had nothing left over to subscribe, must be sad at the ruins of his church. Thus the poor, both bond and free (the mass of the population), would be left without 'the most important relief which it is in our power to bestow', if the churches were not rebuilt.[15]

The Bishop further informed the Governor that in four parishes, churches had been repaired from funds subscribed in the mother country. In St. Michael, the Cathedral and St. Mary's Chapel were wholly or partially repaired; St. Paul's and St. Matthew's Chapels were rebuilt. In St. George, the Parish Church was in large measure repaired and St. Luke's Chapel rebuilt. In St. Andrew and St. James the parish churches were repaired. In the other seven parishes, only the chapels were rebuilt out of these funds. The Bishop argued that the re-erection of the seven parish churches from the remaining portion of the Parliamentary Grant would equalise the award to landholders and other taxable inhabitants throughout the island, place these parishes on the same spiritual footing as the other four, restore the Colony to the ecclesiastical conditions previous to the hurricane, and thus relieve thousands of sufferers.

After the liberal subscriptions that had already been made in the mother country, the Bishop thought that he could not make a second appeal. There was no alternative, so he pressed support for the Resolution of the Commissioners to apply the remaining portion of the Grant to assist in the re construction of the seven parish churches.[16] He won the day and received £7,350 currency from the Parliamentary Hurricane Fund. This contribution enabled him to commence his rebuilding programme, and with other generous subscriptions he was able to complete the restoration of all the parish churches by 1839, at a total cost of £33,745 currency.[17]

In 1834 the Bishop resumed his programme of building Chapels of Ease, and St. Jude was erected in the parish of St. George in that year, with a seating capacity of 400. In 1836 St. Stephen in the parish of St. Michael with accommodation for 530, in 1838 Holy Innocents in the parish of St. Thomas (probably on the site of a chapel destroyed by the hurricane of 1780), seating 500, and in St. Lucy, St. Clement with room for 300 were built. These four new chapels produced additional accommodation for 1,730 worshippers, at a total cost of £4,870 currency, which shows an increase in the cost of providing a chapel.[18] By 1838, therefore, there were ten Chapels of Ease capable of accommodating 5,610 worshippers, striking evidence of the great success of Bishop Coleridge's building programme.

Something must be said about the relation of Chapels of Ease to the parish churches. In 1834 Bishop Coleridge requested the rectors of parishes to define in parishes where Chapels of Ease had been erected the limits of districts where, subject to the superintendence of rectors, the respective clergymen might exclusively exercise their ministry. Such a division of parishes into districts was to be considered as a 'private ecclesiastical arrangement' designed to bring about the more effective execution of ministerial duties. The Curate of a chapel was to reside in his respective district. The Sacraments were to be administered (marriages with the Rector's consent and recommendation), women 'churched' and every other office performed, provided that the incumbents received their 'accustomed fees'. Registers were to be prepared for use in these chapels, kept in a safe place under the sole charge of the respective ministers, and considered as 'parochial' registers, like those of the parish churches. Banns were to be published on the same day both in the Parish Church and in the chapel within the district in which one or both parties resided.[19]

The Chapels of Ease instituted by Bishop Coleridge are of considerable architectural interest. They introduced to the island a new style of ecclesiastical design, the Gothic Revival, especially the Romantic Gothic Revival of the late eighteenth and nineteenth centuries. Some of the characteristics of this Gothic style were the pointed arch and lancet window of which St. Paul's in St. Michael is an untarnished example. It has also been argued that the Gothic style of these chapels had a great influence on later buildings. For example, the Mortuary Chapel in St. John's, a building in the gardens of the then Bay Mansion (close to St. Paul's), some of the churches restored after the hurricane of 1831 (St. John, St. Joseph, and St. Philip with some Gothic characteristics), the Wesleyan chapels of Beulah and Providence. In fact, the 'Coleridge Romantic Gothic Revival Style' became the model for chapel buildings of all denominations in the island for over a century. This was obviously due to his personal knowledge and influence, for in the 'Bishop's Sketch Book', we can see his sketches for Trinity Chapel, St. Mark's Chapel, and St. Paul's (his pride) after the hurricane.[20]

In his Charge of 1834 Bishop Coleridge was able to report that people were flocking to church and there was a great increase in the number of communicants. It was clear to him that he had to provide further accommodation when the enslaved people obtained their full freedom, which was to come in 1838. During the period 1836 to 1842 approximately, he instituted Chapel-Schools and there is evidence that eleven were started: St. Giles, St. Barnabas, St. Lawrence, St. David, St. Martin, St. Catherine, Little St. Joseph, St. Simon, St. Alban, St. Swithin and St. Patrick. Some of these were rebuilt at a later date; for example, Little St. Joseph gave way to the new Chapel of St. Aidan on another site, after the original building collapsed in a landslide. These Chapel-Schools were under the Bishop's license and served as churches on Sundays and schools during the week.[21] They were later consecrated as full chapels when specific Church schools were provided, as we shall see in a later chapter. We do not have a full statement of their seating capacity, but from the figures available we can estimate that they provided accommodation for about 2,400 worshippers.

Additional places must have been provided by St. Saviour and St. Matthias, which were probably instituted in this period as well. On the occasion of laying the corner-stone of St. Barnabas Chapel-School in 1838 the Bishop disclosed in his address that he did not wish it to be like 'St. Matthias, Hastings Village', which was not receiving public support.[22]

There is no doubt that Bishop Coleridge's phenomenal building programme provided a great increase in church accommodation, particularly for the labouring classes. However, as we have seen in the case of St. Mary's above, distinctions were maintained in the seating of Whites and Coloureds in church, and this was to cause some tension, which was to manifest itself as early as 1825. According to one report, 'certain of the coloured people' had left their seats during the Bishop's first Ordination Service, crowded the front and filled up the middle aisle, much to the annoyance of the ladies and gentlemen in the pews. It was further stated that the Coloured and Black people in the gallery were 'conspicuously indecent', and that they should exhibit 'the most beautiful features of the Christian character – meekness and humility'.[23] Another incident was reported by a Coloured man: while he was in church listening to a sermon by Rev. Mr. Payne (St. Andrew's), who appealed for support for Central Schools ('that source of discontent to so many of our colour'), two 'well-dressed' Black men sitting in the front pew of the south gallery annoyed a White lady, making her most uncomfortable.[24]

These incidents reflected the recurrent problem of accommodation in the churches. The pews were reserved for pew-renters; a few places were left open and were normally taken by the Whites. The Free Coloureds and Blacks were relegated to the back of the church and the gallery, and the enslaved were confined to the gallery. When it so happened that there were more Free Coloured and Blacks than there were seats in their section, they would invariably seek to advance into the section reserved for Whites – a section that was invariably spacious and underutilised – rather than share the already crowded and 'inferior' (though elevated) portion occupied by the enslaved people.

It was inevitable that the question of pew-rental would loom large and the Bishop would have to face it head on. In March 1825 a controversy over this practice raged in the *Barbadian*. One 'Rumpus' wrote, deploring the right to own pews in the Cathedral, which practice could not be justified either politically or religiously. He mentioned that pews were transferred from one person to another, and that some people were furious if others sat in their pews. He questioned whether such persons were religious. He went on to observe that the innovation of having people face the clergy, by making single pews adaptable to the climate, was very discomforting, especially for the ladies. He felt that 'our distinguished friend on the hill' (the Bishop) and the 'respectable and the rational' inhabitants were hugging the *status quo* in this matter of seating in church.

The Editor, in an appended comment, defended the Establishment by stating that the proposal to overthrow the 'long established rights of the occupants of pews' would be most disruptive; that the new arrangements concerning the owners of pews were concluded in June 1823 by the Vestry, and that since the arrival of the Lord Bishop many persons, long absent from church, had returned to church. The Editor went on to suggest that what was needed was another church.[25]

In a letter of 17 March, a layman argued that the accommodation in the Cathedral was inadequate, so that numerous families in Town and the environs were unable to attend church. He thought that nothing should be done to impede the increase of accommodation, and that the Vestry should take the necessary steps. The Editor again defended the pew-rental system and suggested that the subject be dropped. He also sent a letter to the Bishop signed by himself, the Churchwarden and Vestrymen. They informed the Bishop that from the Minutes of the Vestry it appeared that after the storm of 1780 pew-rental was introduced to help meet the cost of rebuilding the church, two persons being asked to pay each £7.10, £6, or £5, according to the size and position of the pews. Such pews were owned by the purchaser or his heirs, and could be disposed of as freehold property. Some transfers of pews were made to the exclusion of 'many respectable Householders now resident in the Parish', causing much dissatisfaction. It was therefore the desire of the Rector, Churchwarden and Vestry to throw open the Cathedral as public property in order to advance the worship of Almighty God.[26]

As far as they could glean from the Minutes, the then Ordinary had not been consulted nor did he approve the sale of pews, which approval was necessary if one were to be given the right to sit in a particular pew in church. They could also cite 'a learned Author in Ecclesiastical Affairs', that a seat in church could not be granted by the Ordinary to a person and his heirs absolutely, for the seat did not belong to the 'person' but to the 'inhabitant'. If this position were accepted, they thought that they could plan to refund the original holders of pews, not their heirs or assignees.[27] As they saw it, the matter of the right to own pews had originated at a time when the Rector, Churchwarden and Vestry were seeking funds to rebuild and refurnish the Parish Church of St. Michael after the storm of 1780.

The Bishop himself expressed some concern about pew-rental in the Cathedral. He observed in 1825 that it did not offer public accommodation, since the pews were private property, 'so that neither officers nor their families and still less the soldiery can avail themselves on the Sabbath of the British Church'.[28] However, he was very cautious in dealing with this matter, and in fact he concentrated more on increasing accommodation by providing additional seats and buildings rather than on discarding the pew-rental system. He obviously encouraged his clergy to adopt this procedure. He sent a questionnaire to his clergy concerning additional accommodation in their respective churches and chapels. The Rectors of St. George, St. John, St. Lucy and St. Michael reported that no additional accommodation had been provided in their churches. The Rectors of Christ Church and St. Thomas had provided some additional benches for the use of the Coloured congregations, while the Vestry of St. Philip, at the request of the Rector, had ordered additional seats to be provided in the galleries for the enslaved people. The Rector of St. Andrew had provided additional seats for about 60 children; the Rectors of St. Joseph and St. Peter had placed benches in the aisles of their churches. The Rector of St. James gave the ambiguous reply that 'Every accommodation has been provided, that the church will admit'.[29] The Rectors were obviously not too enthusiastic about increasing accommodation in their parish churches.

In 1834 the Bishop gave his opinion that seats in church and chapel were for inhabitants, so that they might more conveniently attend Divine Service. He also stated that the use of such seats was common to all who paid for their repairs; that the responsibility for appointing persons to seats lay with the Ordinary, so that there be no contention. In the whole matter of pew rental, he disclosed that he was prepared to follow the law of Britain.[30] In Britain, however, legal opinion was divided on this matter. According to one opinion, the Churchwarden had no right 'to displace parishioners already possessing seats according to their rank and quality', for although money and rent did not give them 'title', yet they were parishioners 'in possession', and therefore had 'possessory rights' independent of payment.[31] According to another opinion, the sale, and purchase, of pews in parish churches was invalid and illegal; only in chapels which were private property was such a practice possible. Further, the churchwardens were responsible for the disposal of seats in church, acting as officers of the Bishop with whom the apportioning of seats ultimately rested. If seats were not being used, the churchwardens could dispose of them by placing other parishioners in them.[32]

As we have seen above, this latter interpretation, that the apportioning of seating in church was the ultimate responsibility of the Bishop, was understood by Bishop Coleridge. He obviously did not exercise this right in respect of the pew-rental system in the parish churches, but chose rather to increase accommodation by provision of other places of worship.

On another matter, it seemed to have been the custom to hold elections in the parish churches for members to serve in the General Assembly and for members of the vestries. In 1838 an Act was passed to stop this practice. Instead of in churches, chapels and licensed places of worship, elections for the General Assembly, or of vestrymen for the parish of St. Michael, should henceforth be held in the Town Hall, Bridgetown, and all elections for other parishes in such convenient places as the churchwardens for the time being would provide. If there was no appropriate parochial building, then the churchwardens would have power to hire one at a cost to the parish, and give notice of the appointed place at least 21 days before the elections.[33] From this measure it is clear that the churches and chapels were to be used for public worship, and for such educational purposes as were determined by the Bishop, and under his licence.

Bishop Coleridge showed tremendous administrative acumen in mobilising and deploying the physical resources of the Church in Barbados. Towards the end of his episcopate (1841), there were approximately 22,500 seats for worship, of which some 10,116 were provided by his programme of erecting new places of worship and the remarkable rebuilding scheme which he undertook after the terrible hurricane of 1831. There were some 9,155 worshippers utilising these additional seats, thereby indicating that there was a demand for additional accommodation in town and country. Compared with figures for public worship, the number of communicants tended to be low. The average was 14 per cent of those attending worship on Sunday over the whole island. A few churches showed an attendance of communicants of around 25 per cent, for example, St. Michael's (Cathedral), St. Mary's, and St. Paul's; whereas at the other end of the scale were

St. Simon's and St. Andrew's. The population of the island at this time was about 120,000. The figure of 22,500 seats for worshippers represents, therefore, just over 17 per cent of the population, a not insignificant figure when one considers that the population included children, and no distinction was now made among Whites, long-term Free Coloureds and recently freed Blacks.[34] In his use of Chapel-Schools for the dual purpose of worship and education, to meet the challenge of 'the vast numbers of our brethren who are arriving at civil freedom, but are yet very careless about the bondage of sin',[35] the Bishop showed both innovative imagination and decisiveness.

# 4

# THE MINISTRY
## ADMINISTRATION, RECRUITMENT AND THEOLOGICAL EDUCATION

BISHOP COLERIDGE'S IMAGINATION AND energies were no less in evidence in his administration of the human resources to meet the task of amelioration and evangelisation in his new diocese. Before he left for Barbados he saw to it that provision was made for two archdeacons to assist him with the administration of his far-flung diocese. Early in his episcopate he also instituted the office of Rural Dean to have local oversight in a defined area. He increased the ranks of his clergy by recruitment from the universities of Oxford and Cambridge and from Trinity College, Dublin, having settled the question of Colonial Ordination before he left England.

However, he realised that if there was to be a settled and continued ministry – particularly among the labouring classes – he would need to recruit local candidates for the Sacred Ministry and make provision locally for their training. He therefore turned his special attention to the re-organisation of Codrington College in accordance with the intentions of the testator, Christopher Codrington. In addition to making provision for the recruitment and training of local clergy, he also instituted the ministry of readers and catechists to supplement that of the clergy. The Bishop was also concerned about adequate financial support of his ministers, and to this end he secured increases in salary for the clergy.

When it was intimated to him that he would be nominated to the new

See proposed by His Majesty's Government, Coleridge gave immediate thought to the selection of two archdeacons, each of whom would receive a salary of £1,500 sterling (£2,000 currency). He envisaged that the archdeacons would have a period of service like his own – twelve years – and would receive a small pension on retirement. He wrote to his friend, the Rev. John Keble, then a Fellow of Oriel College, Oxford, concerning all this. He informed Keble that he was looking for an 'able co-adjutor' to work with him in 'so great and good a cause', and was not losing a moment in making Keble the offer of one of the Archdeaconries.[1] Keble refused the offer because of his father's failing health.[2]

This refusal was obviously a great disappointment to Coleridge, and from Keble's later inquiries concerning him it is clear that no correspondence passed between them for a number of years. 'How is Wm. Coleridge going on?' '... How is W. Coleridge now?' '... I am anxious to hear how they go on in Barbados after the dreadful calamity they had endured.'[3] Keble was, however, able to arrange for his Oriel colleague, the Rev. Richard Hurrell Froude, to go to Barbados, and become domestic Chaplain to Bishop Coleridge in 1834. In that same year the Bishop consulted Keble concerning a successor to the Rev. John Hothersall Pinder, who was to retire from the principalship of Codrington College in 1835. By this time, therefore, communication had been renewed between two trusted friends.[4]

Following Keble's refusal of his private offer, Coleridge had to look elsewhere for his archdeacons. He was formally informed by Lord Bathurst that Archdeaconries should be constituted in the new Sees in the West Indies in accordance with the procedure in other colonial Sees: His Majesty's Letters Patent would be issued, founding the Archdeaconries and appointing persons to fill them; the Bishop would also be given power to collate to these offices (after 'the death-or other avoidance' of the archdeacons first appointed) persons selected by the Bishop, previously recommended by the Secretary of State and approved by His Majesty the King who reserved the right of revoking or cancelling such appointments.[5] (It was also stipulated that, in addition to the customary 'Fees of Office' to be paid from public funds upon the issuing of Letters Patent for Archdeaconries in the West Indies, a stamp duty, according to the emoluments of the office, was to be paid under the Act of the 55 George 3d, cap. 184, by the person accepting the appointment. The scale was set out as follows:

Emoluments from £1,500 to £2,000: £100 duty

Emoluments from £2,000 to £3,000: £150 duty

Emoluments from £3,000 and upwards: £200 duty

Each new Archdeacon for the West Indies would thus have to pay £100 duty.[6]

In 1825 the Letters Patent were issued, instituting 'one Archdeaconry in and over the Islands of Barbados, Grenada, Saint Vincent, Trinidad, Tobago, Saint Lucia, and their respective Dependencies, to be styled the Archdeaconry of Barbados; and also one other Archdeaconry in and over the Islands of Antigua, Montserrat, Dominica, Saint Christopher, Nevis, and the Virgin Islands, and their respective Dependencies, to be styled the Archdeaconry of Antigua', to be subject to the Bishop's See of Barbados and the Leeward Islands.

By the same Letters the Rev. Edward Eliot and the Rev. Thomas Parry were nominated and appointed Archdeacons of Barbados and Antigua respectively, subject to the powers of revocation and of resignation. Bishop Coleridge was then authorised to institute the two archdeacons to assist him and have such jurisdiction as would be determined by him. Also, at their deaths or 'other avoidance', the Bishop would have the right to collate their successors, after recommendation by one of the Principal Secretaries of State and approval by His Majesty, and his heirs and successors.[7] So when Bishop Coleridge arrived in Barbados, he already had the appointment of his archdeacons settled and he could proceed to administer his large Diocese with able assistants.

Bishop Coleridge also had to provide local oversight of the 'Colonies and settlements of Demerara, Essequibo and Berbice, and their dependencies', which were annexed to the See of Barbados and the Leeward Islands by Letters Patent in 1826. For this portion of his Diocese in British Guiana, he chose to appoint a Commissary. The Rev. J.H. Pinder's ministry as Chaplain on the Codrington Estates greatly impressed the Bishop who made him his Chaplain and sent him as Commissary to British Guiana in 1827. Later the Rev. William Piercy Austin was appointed Ecclesiastical Commissary of British Guiana. He ably administered it (the three counties of Demerara, Essequibo and Berbice),[8] and was subsequently collated as its Archdeacon by Bishop Coleridge.

In order to strengthen his administration further at the local base, Bishop Coleridge instituted the office of Rural Dean, as was the practice in England. A Rural Dean had power and charge of the country parishes; he was assigned and directed by the Bishop and Archdeacon. His duty was to give account of the 'lives and manners' of the clergy under his care, to convene the clergy within his Deanery, and to induct clergy to benefices in the absence of the Archdeacon. He also had to submit the returns, inspect churches, chancels, chapels, parsonages and vicarages, and report on them.[9]

By 1835 Bishop Coleridge had appointed six rural deans: the Honourable and Rev. J.H. Gittens, Rector of St. John (Barbados); the Rev. Robert Holberton (Antigua); the Honourable and Rev. D.G. Davis (St. Christopher's); the Rev. J. Checkley (St. Vincent); the Rev. J.C. Baker (Grenada); and the Rev. T.R. Redwar (Berbice).[10] By 1839, to this list was added the Rev. George Cummins, Rural Dean of Trinidad.[11] Bishop Coleridge clearly saw that it was important to delegate authority, not only because his Diocese ranged widely, but also that the ordering of the Church's ministry might be effective at the local level.

The number of clergy ministering in Barbados on Bishop Coleridge's arrival was fifteen. There were eleven rectors of the parish churches, a minister at All Saints' Chapel, the Master of the Central School in Bridge Town, the Chaplain on the Codrington Estates and the Acting Principal of Codrington College.[12] The Bishop expressed some concern about the poor health of the Rector of St. Peter, the Rev. James Neblett, which had resulted in the declining state of the parish.[13] Neblett was later succeeded by the Rev. W.P. Hinds (Rector of St. Joseph).[14]

The Bishop had a great admiration for the ministry of the Rev. J.H. Pinder on the Codrington Estates, and for the whole re-organisation of Codrington College, in which Finder also featured prominently. The Bishop had also noted the work of the Rev. John Packer, Master of the Central School in St. Michael, in which parish good leadership was given by the Rector, the Rev. William Garnett.

The ministry of the Rev. William Harte, Rector of St. Lucy, and his relationship with the Bishop, is worthy of separate mention. William Harte was born in Barbados on 25 November 1776. He was educated at the Free School in Bridgetown where he himself subsequently kept a school from about 1796 to 1800. In the latter year Harte went to England to offer himself to the Bishop of London as a candidate for Holy Orders. He was made a deacon on Sunday, 23 November and ordained priest a week later, and returned to Barbados.

Even before ordination he had been offered a title as Curate of St. Michael's by the Rector. In this cure he served diligently, particularly among the Coloured population. In 1801 he accepted the appointment of assistant to the Rev. Mark Nicholson, Principal of Codrington College. He served as schoolmaster to the White pupils of the College and catechist to the enslaved people on the estates. In 1804 he was appointed Rector of St. Joseph, and in 1815 became the Rector of St. Lucy. In this parish he was determined to minister to the labouring class. He recommended to the congregation the religious instruction of enslaved people. With the initial support of proprietors and one overseer, over 300 enslaved people attended his Wednesday evening lectures. This lecture programme was disrupted in 1820, but re-introduced in 1821, first on Sunday afternoons and then on Wednesday afternoons. The numbers had, however, declined, as more and more pressure was put on Harte and his endeavours by his White parishioners.

The storm burst on Easter Day, 15 April 1825, when William Harte preached a sermon which his White parishioners considered most offensive, as he dared to express the doctrine of equality. He also intensified their fury by administering communion to the enslaved people, without allowing the customary interval of time for the Whites to retire from the altar. At a public meeting on 21 April, the White parishioners resolved to take action against Harte for '... endeavouring to alienate their slaves from a sense of their duty by inculcating doctrines of equality inconsistent with their obedience to their masters and the policy of the island'. The matter was taken to Bishop Coleridge who upheld Harte's defence of his action. Incensed that no satisfaction was given by the Bishop, the Churchwarden and Vestry of the parish took the matter to the civil courts, and when the magistrates failed to agree, it was taken to the Court of Grand Sessions, which found Harte guilty and fined him 'one shilling'.

Bishop Coleridge acted on Harte's behalf and secured him 'a royal pardon'. The Secretary of State for the Colonies declared the case closed after some complaints were made in a local newspaper, the *Globe*, supported by the House of Assembly. In 1831 the Bishop transferred Harte to the Cathedral as Curate, and in 1832 gave him the cure of St. Mary's. Harte also served as one of the Bishop's chaplains, and distinguished himself for his sermons and lectures. He died on 11 January 1851, and a monument to him can be seen in St. Mary's Church.[15]

We have looked at the life and ministry of William Harte in some detail, because of his willingness to challenge the *status quo* and to preach the Gospel to bond and free alike. It is significant to note that he was a White native of Barbados. It is true that there is no evidence that he advocated the abolition of enslavement, but he was conspicuous in his endeavours to incorporate the enslaved people into the body of worship of the Church and to extend pastoral care to them. He was the only minister to perform a marriage between enslaved persons before 1825.[16] He took a stand against the Sunday dances of the enslaved people in St. Lucy, established a system of catechetical instruction for them on the plantations in that parish and was able to employ a Sunday schoolmaster for them.[17] It can be said that for Harte, civilisation and evangelisation went hand in hand in his ministry among the enslaved people. His policy met the approval of the new Bishop who vindicated him from the charges of his White accusers, and transferred him to a strategic place for influencing the development of the ministry of the Church among the coloured population.

Bishop Coleridge would have been greatly encouraged if other rectors had shown Harte's zeal for the religious upliftment of the enslaved people. He must have seen very early that he had to recruit local candidates for the ministry. For the time being, however, he had to continue recruiting candidates from Britain.

As previously mentioned, before he left England he had settled the question of Colonial Ordination. He had received the opinion of Dr. Stephen Lushington, on behalf of the Doctors Commons, that the Bishopric of Barbados was established by Letters Patent and that the Bishop of Barbados had the same general ecclesiastical jurisdiction in his Diocese as English bishops had in theirs. In any case, the See of Barbados and the Leeward Islands was in the Province of Canterbury, to whose Archbishop the Bishop had taken the oath of canonical obedience at his consecration. Lushington then referred to the two specific questions raised by the Bishop: (i) 'Whether an Englishman, having taken a degree at Oxford, and being ordained by the Bishop of Barbados within his Diocese, can, upon his return to England, hold preferment in this country'; (ii) 'Whether a native of Barbados, ordained there, can, on coming to England, hold preferment there'.

Lushington gave his opinion that the answer to the first question was in the affirmative, and that, with regard to the second question, 'a native of Barbados stands in the same legal situation as an Englishman born'. Lushington further stated that he had examined the Patent and could find no prohibiting clauses. Also, he knew of no law or statute that would prevent such persons from holding preferment in England.[18] Coleridge's questions, and the judgement they evoked from the Doctors Commons, might have had far-reaching significance. In 1829 it was reported that an Act of Parliament had laid down that 'no person . . . who shall have been ordained by a colonial Bishop, who, at the time of such ordination did not actually possess an episcopal jurisdiction over some Diocese, district, or place, shall be capable in any way, or on any pretence whatever . . . of officiating as a minister of the established Church of England. . . .'[19] The way had thus been paved for Bishop Coleridge to recruit clergy from Britain.

Bishop Coleridge ordained his first English recruits on 13 February 1825. To the priesthood he ordained Mr. Bryan Taylor Nurse, BA, Queen's College, Oxford, who had been made a deacon in England, and to the diaconate he admitted Mr. Richard Caddy Thomas, SCL, Exeter College, Oxford. During that first year of his episcopate, the Bishop ordained to the priesthood four who had been made deacons in England, and to the diaconate he admitted two candidates, all graduates of Oxford colleges.[20] The Bishop continued to recruit candidates mainly from the universities of Oxford and Cambridge and from Trinity College, Dublin, to meet the needs of his far-flung Diocese.[21]

Early in his episcopate, however, Bishop Coleridge saw that he could not continue to rely on clergy coming from Britain, particularly as many of them fell victim to the climate and to some social vices. He was determined that a good number of native clergy be trained. So he unflinchingly turned his mind to re-organising Codrington College so that theological education might be firmly established there, in accordance with the intention of the testator, Christopher Codrington.

Christopher Codrington was born in Barbados in 1668. His father, Sir Christopher Codrington, was successively a member of Council and Deputy Governor of Barbados, and later Captain-General of the Leeward Islands.

His grandfather, also Christopher Codrington, had obtained land in St. John's Parish and had become very wealthy. Christopher Codrington III was educated in England, and matriculated at Christ Church, Oxford, as a Gentleman-Commoner on 4 July 1685. Leaving Christ Church, he was elected to a Fellowship at All Souls College, Oxford, in 1690; obtained the BA in 1691; and subsequently became distinguished for his poetic and literary gifts. In 1694–95 he was granted the MA.[22]

Four years after his election to All Souls he served under King William III in Flanders, while retaining his Fellowship, and was present at the siege of Namur. The King showed his appreciation of his gallantry, and the outstanding services of his father, by appointing him to succeed his father as Captain-General and Governor of the Leeward Islands. It was just before he led an expedition against the French in Guadeloupe in 1703 that Christopher Codrington wrote his Will, bequeathing his two inherited sugar estates in Barbados – Society and Consett – in trust to the SPG (which was founded in 1701) as follows:

> I give and bequeathe my two plantations in the Island of Barbados, to the Society for the Propagation of the Christian Religion in Foreign Parts, erected . . . by my late good master, King William III; and my desire is to have the plantations continue entire, and three hundred negroes, at least, always kept thereon; and a convenient number of Professors and Scholars maintained there; all of them to be under vows of poverty, chastity and obedience; who shall be obliged to study and practice Physic and Chirurgery, as well as divinity; that by the apparent usefulness of the former to all mankind, they may both endear themselves to the people, and have the better opportunities of doing good to men's souls, whilst they are taking care of their bodies; but the particulars of the constitution I leave to the Society composed of wise and good men.[23]

After Christopher Codrington's death on the 7 April 1710, the SPG had some legal difficulties with the executor of the Will, Lieutenant-Colonel William Codrington. However, by 1712 the estates in Barbados passed into their hands. Christopher's Will had reflected his desire that enslaved people be converted to Christianity and that for them salvation should be total, of bodies as well as of souls. In a later chapter we shall see how the SPG provided catechists for the religious instruction and pastoral care of the enslaved people on the Codrington Estates.

With regard to the educational aspect of the bequest, the SPG first founded Codrington College in 1745 as a Grammar School whose aim was to educate the sons of 'gentlemen', who were given exhibitions to further their studies in British universities. In 1819 the SPG instituted an allowance of £100 from the Trust funds at the Grammar School, to be granted annually for four years to those of the twelve Foundation Scholars who wished to further their studies in England, in Divinity, Law or Physic. It is interesting to note that Edward Parris Smith, who was later Tutor of Codrington College, was one of those who benefited from this generous provision.[24]

Under constant attack from anti-slavery leaders, the SPG reverted to the Codrington bequest with a view to establishing theological education at the College, according to the intention of the testator. They had implicit trust in Bishop Coleridge who also was enthusiastic that the wishes of Christopher Codrington be fulfilled, particularly as he himself hoped that his programme of educating and evangelising the enslaved people population would be advanced by the training of indigenous clergy at the College. Encouraged by the excellent financial yield from the estates, and egged on by the Bishop, the SPG reported in 1825 as follows:

> The prosperous state of their affairs encouraged the Society to take into consideration the practicability of placing the College upon a more respectable footing; one more conformable to the intentions of the testator, and their own original views ... with these views a plan had been formed for giving it the character of a University, and arrangements have been under consideration for securing to it the services of a Principal and two or three Professors. By these means an adequate education may be provided for such of the West Indian youths as are disposed to devote themselves to the Christian Ministry within their native islands without the expense and trouble of seeking the necessary qualifications in Europe, at a distance from their friends and relations. This important measure could not be carried into full execution without the effectual aid of His Majesty's Government; not only under the sanction of the civil authorities, but by a liberal grant of money. And the Society are encouraged to believe, from the cordial approbation with which the plan was entertained, that the countenance and co-operation of Government will not be wanting when the arrangements are in progress. The first step will be to enlarge the buildings, so as to render them capable of containing a sufficient number of students; and the plans and estimates for this purpose are now under consideration; and it is confidently expected that the Society will be

able to report considerable progress in this most interesting work in the abstract for the following year.[25]

In 1829, on his return from England, the Bishop informed the clergy of the Diocese about the new plans for Codrington College. He disclosed that it would primarily be a 'Theological Institution' for the education of students of 'Divinity', but the College would be made 'as generally useful to Students in all professions, as circumstances may require and funds allow'. The Bishop of the Diocese was appointed Visitor by the Society.

The Society had also appointed as Principal a person in whom the Bishop had absolute confidence, the Rev. John Hothersall Pinder, who was born in Barbados, educated in England and was a Master of Arts of Cambridge University. Pinder had also proved himself an able and faithful priest as Chaplain on the Codrington Estates, Curate of St. Mary's, Bridgetown, and the Bishop's Ecclesiastical Commissary in British Guiana. For a regional institution he was also qualified, since he had visited every part of the Diocese. Edward Parris Smith, appointed Tutor, had graduated from Pembroke College, Oxford, with a BA, and was subsequently granted the MA. He was made a deacon in England and was ordained priest by the Bishop on the 28 December 1829. To join this team, the Society was securing the services of Dr. James Dotten Maycock, MD, as Medical Professor.[26]

With regard to the student body, the Bishop further informed the clergy that twelve young men would be received as Foundation Exhibitioners, with free tuition, board and lodging. These exhibitions would be open, for competition, to all young men intended for the Church throughout the British West Indies. The non-Foundation students would have to pay a moderate sum for their tuition, board and lodging. When the improvements of the existing buildings were completed, accommodation would be provided for fourteen students. The Society was prepared to erect an additional wing if the number of applicants warranted it. The Lodge of the Rev. John Packer, formerly Master of the Central School and now Chaplain on the estates, had become the new location of the school previously kept at the College. At this school six boys, duly recommended 'from any British West India Colony', would be boarded and educated in the classical languages,

> free of cost to their parents, and 'at a fit age' they would be eligible to compete for any vacant exhibition at the College. The Bishop observed that since many

young persons in the West Indies could not complete their education in England, and since a sound course of study was essential for future 'Stewards of God's Word', the Diocese would benefit greatly from Codrington College as a theological institution, from which would graduate 'able and faithful Ministers'.[27]

On 30 June 1829 the Principal and Tutor commenced theological education at their private residences near Bridgetown, as the College was undergoing extensive repairs. They gave lectures to four young Barbadians who desired to offer themselves as candidates for Holy Orders, and had been nominated by the Civil Authorities who were Governors of the College. In 1830 these four were joined by other candidates, bringing the total to twenty-six.[28] It was a moment of great rejoicing when the College buildings were completed and the College was formally opened on 9 September 1830, the anniversary of the opening of the Grammar School in 1745.[29] The sentiments expressed in the *Barbadian* are worthy of note:

> the earnest labours of his Lordship to spread far and wide the inestimable blessings of the Gospel – the warm interest he has ever evinced in the spiritual and temporal welfare of the immense population of souls committed to his charge – and especially the arduous and persevering exertions he has made to encourage and promote the instruction of youth – are circumstances so well known to all, that it would be a work of supererogation in us now to enlarge upon them. Every friend to Religion – God's best gift to man – every true patriot, must rejoice at the good which has been effected, and should pray fervently for the continuance of a heavenly blessing on the labour of all those who devote their time and talents to the furtherance of Christian doctrine, and the encouragement of Christian practice.[30]

The *Barbadian* further reported that, thanks to the unwearied exertions of the Lord Bishop, the College was opened with the Bishop himself as Visitor, and under the noble Principal and distinguished professors would reach 'a lofty eminence as a seat of learning'.[31]

The great significance of the opening of Codrington College, as a college for theological education in Barbados, and for the Barbadian society as a whole, can be seen from the description of the opening ceremony. In the official assembly were the Bishop, the Principal, the Tutor and the Medical Professor, accompanied by the Governor, the Archdeacon and clergy of the island. The 'young gentlemen exhibitioners' in their caps and gowns and the Commoners in their sleeveless gowns led the procession. Also present were the Honourable Speaker, the Honourable Attorney and Solicitor Generals, who with the Governor and President of the Council had hitherto been *virtute officii* Governors of the College. In the gathering too were ladies and several members of His Majesty's Council and of the House of Assembly, as well as Forster Clarke, Esq., the 'faithful and able attorney of the Society in England' (SPG), Dr. Hinkson, 'the judicious and humane manager of the properties' (Codrington Estates), a large number of 'gentlemen' from various parts of the island and officers of His Majesty's Army. This was indeed a State gathering.

After an extract from Christopher Codrington's bequest had been read, the Bishop declared the names of the Exhibitioners, the Principal read the matriculation entries, and an appeal was made for Ordinands who would be duly certified by ministers of their respective parishes. Extracts from the Minutes of the meeting of the Committee of the SPG, 8 December 1828, were also read, disclosing that the Governors of the College had been empowered to nominate four Foundation Scholars as candidates for Holy Orders, and the Bishop, as Visitor, had the power to nominate eight Exhibitioners, all 'subject to such examination as the Visitor shall deem expedient'.[32]

Later in September the Bishop reported to SPG on the first examination that had been held:

(Nominated by the Bishop)

*First Class*
 W.W. Jackson
 K.B. Skeete
 J.A. Barclay
 F.R. Brathwaite

(Nominated by the Civil Authorities who had acted as Governors of the College)

*Second Class*
 J.A. Anton
 J.M. Pearn

G.F. Sealy
F.B. Grant
R.H. Barrow
J.H. Gittens

(Nominated by the Civil Authorities)

*Third Class*

D. Gittens
S.P. Musson
Mills
T.R. Redwar
J. Hobson
J.N. Garland
J.A. Gittens
W.A. Beckles
J.A. Bascom[33]

Besides the Exhibitioners, as mentioned above, some gentlemen were nominated as 'Commoners', who had passed a 'good examination' and would pay a moderate sum for their board, but would be granted free lodging. The Bishop thought that the expenses for the 'Commoners' would not exceed £40 sterling per annum.[34] The Bishop also expressed the view that 'at no distant day, therefore, we may now expect that this College will supply the Diocese with a body of native clergy instructed in the best principles, and trained in the best discipline that the munificence of its founder and the wisdom of its governors could devise'.[35]

There is evidence in the episcopate of Coleridge that the word 'native' theoretically included 'coloured' or 'Negro' as far as candidates for Holy Orders in the Diocese were concerned. In fact, there is evidence that his Archdeacon, Parry, who was to succeed him as Bishop of Barbados, suggested in 1842 that Exhibitions be provided at the College for candidates for Holy Orders – 'men of colour' who would 'go to the Coast of Africa'.[36]

The actual opening of term had to be deferred until 12 October 1830 because additional accommodation had to be provided, by further repairs to the College, to meet the number of applicants, which had grown to eighteen. Mills, mentioned above, did not enter the College, nor did some of those who began in 1829. By 1830, with the opening of the College and the previous course of lectures given by the Principal and Tutor, thirty-one students had begun to benefit from its re-organisation. Of these, twenty-two were Barbadians. The College, however, had a regional dimension from the beginning, as students came from other islands in the Diocese (Antigua, Montserrat, Dominica and Trinidad). Also, one student came from Bermuda and two from England.[37]

The high expectations raised by the opening were initially frustrated by the terrible hurricane of 1831 which caused havoc in the island. The College and the estates' buildings were almost completely destroyed. With generous contributions from the SPG and SPCK, however, the College and other buildings were soon restored.[38] The work of the College continued. On 16 December 1832, the Bishop ordained one of his first Barbadian recruits to the priesthood, Samuel Rous Moe Brathwaite, whom he had made deacon on 6 January of the same year. Brathwaite was one of the first students who had received lectures at the residences of the Principal and Tutor.

Another candidate who was ordained at the same time was Henry Newton Gage Hall, a Trinidadian who had joined the first batch of students to be given lectures.[39] In 1834 the Bishop could report that of the number of the clergy in the Diocese, which had increased to seventy-three, four were from 'our own College'. He also reported that twenty students were at the College, the majority of whom were preparing for Holy Orders, and he was very satisfied with 'our diocesan institution'. He stated further that he was most encouraged by the assurance given by the SPG that they would spare no effort in maintaining 'the present establishment of Codrington'.[40] By 1835 the Bishop had ordained seven of those candidates who had begun their studies in 1829 and five of those who had begun with the opening of the College in 1830.[41] When Principal Pinder was obliged to resign in 1835 because of ill-health, forty-nine students had passed through his hands since 1829, and twenty-seven of these were ordained.[42]

He was succeeded by the Rev. Henry Jones, MA, of Exeter College, Oxford. From 1830 to 1842 some eighty-seven students were admitted to the College, fifty-nine of whom were Barbadians. The College had admitted students not only from all other parts of the Diocese, but had also attracted students from England, Ireland and New Brunswick.[43] The number of clergy in Barbados grew from fifteen to twenty-nine during Coleridge's episcopate. One graduate of Codrington had become Rector of the parish of Christ Church, the Rev. C.C. Gill, who had been one of the first students of the College. But it seems to have been the Bishop's policy to appoint Barbadian graduates of the College to serve in other parts of the Diocese.[44]

While the students were in training, the Bishop appointed them to serve as readers in chapels and places of worship, under the supervision of rectors. The Bishop requested that they should devote most of Sunday to this assignment. Most students, therefore, left the College on Saturday evenings and visited 'as many estates as possible in the more remote parishes' to assist with Sunday Schools and to prepare adults for baptism.[45] A report by one of the first students, W.W. Jackson, Reader at Claybury Estate, St. John, gives a good picture of the work of a Reader. He had visited the estate on Sunday, 5 December 1830, and had visited regularly since that date, thanks to the co-operation of the proprietor, Mr. Sharp. Jackson then described the 7 a.m. Service: the children sang the morning hymn, after which the Reader conducted the Service, composed of prayers from the liturgy and a lecture, all lasting one hour.

The congregation dispersed, while the adult candidates for baptism and the children remained. These were divided into three classes of young people, totalling about 100; the adults comprised a separate class. The children were examined in the Church Catechism, while the adults were instructed in those parts of the Catechism required by rubric to be known in preparation for baptism. The children stayed on for breakfast and afterwards reassembled in three classes for the 'business of the Sunday Reading School (on the National Plan)'. The class teachers were the 'apprenticed' on the estate and two of the enslaved labourers who could read reasonably well. The Reader remained an hour, supervising and assisting the teachers. The 'business' went on until 1 o'clock.

The aggregate number of enslaved people on the estate was 213, and the average number of the congregation was 145, which Jackson did not regard as satisfactory, considering that the proprietor gave a day in reward to those who attended for three successive Sundays. To date, the Reader had presented thirteen adults and sixty children to the Rector for baptism, and almost all the enslaved people on that property were admitted 'into covenant with God'.[46] From this account we see that the services of the students of the College, as readers, had become very significant in the religious education of the enslaved population.

In 1834 the Bishop publicly lauded the work of the Readers whom he considered 'auxiliaries' to the 'parochial and regular clergy'. By assembling the young and the adults on the plantations and elsewhere for worship and instruction, and by teaching the young 'the letters' so that they could learn to read what the clergy would more fully explain, the readers were to be commended for their work. In the Bishop's opinion they were removing ignorance and preparing the parishioners to be more holy. Also, they were qualifying themselves for a more effective discharge of their future ministry. The Bishop clearly saw the work of a reader as an integral part of a student's training. The 'necessity of devotion and discipline in life and studies' would be learnt, and the student would also find that 'now is the time to lay up stores of theological and pastoral information'.[47]

In addition to the clergy and readers, the Bishop established the Order of Catechists in the Diocese to provide religious instruction on the plantations. The ministry of catechists had already been introduced to the Codrington Estates by the SPG since the appointment of the 'medical missionary', the Rev. Joseph Holt, in 1713 as the 'Society's Chaplain, Catechist & Supervisor of the Sick and maimed Servants and Negroes'. This catechetical system was to continue until early in the nineteenth century, with an oscillation between partial success and frustration, and certainly in the face of much opposition from the Abolitionists in England, who constantly attacked the SPG for attempting to prove that slavery and Christianity were compatible.[48]

Bishop Coleridge, however, considered the ministry of catechists vital for the Church's outreach to the enslaved population. Catechists were to be licensed by him after due subscription and examination; they would be placed under the supervision of parochial clergy, and would consult with the proprietors of the several plantations concerning the appropriate times of instruction.[49] The instructions were to be determined by the Bishop or selected by the respective clergy out of the SPCK catalogue. The Bishop was able to report that he had licensed catechists in St. Thomas, St. James and St. Andrew, and proposed, as funds permitted, to place one or more in each parish. For funding, he made an appeal to all interested persons and proposed to form a Branch Association of the Society for the Conversion of Blacks. In this he succeeded, and there was a good response to his appeal. He then proposed to establish a Catechetical Fund, to be supplemented by funds from England and by monies placed at his disposal by His Majesty's Government. In this way, he thought, a sufficient number of catechists would be provided for the island of Barbados.[50]

The Bishop required that catechists be able to read, be instructed in psalmody and be competent to explain to Blacks any word or passage of Scripture.[51] Before they were appointed by the Bishop, they had to declare that they would only teach and read in plantations that which the 'Minister of the Parish' directed for the instruction of 'the young and ignorant in the principles of the Christian religion'; that they could visit plantations and other places at the times agreed upon by the minister and the respective proprietors; that they would dress soberly for the occasion, would give no cause for offence, but promote concord; that they would be diligent in reading the Holy Scriptures, 'with prayer and good advisement', to increase their knowledge; and that they would report weekly, or as often as the minister required, on the number and names of the plantations they had visited and the spiritual progress made thereon.[52]

In 1834 the Bishop publicly expressed his pleasure that a 'considerable body' of readers and catechists had been appointed to act as 'auxiliaries' to the clergy. They were commended for their ministry of preparing both young and old to profit from the ministrations of the clergy. As the Bishop saw it, the services of catechists were not limited to Sunday, but extended throughout the week. They should be satisfied with the privilege of carrying from estate to estate 'that instruction so long withheld', gathering 'the lambs of Christ's flock' and 'teaching their almost infant tongues to lisp the name of the Redeemer'.[53] The work of a catechist had become significant in the religious education of the enslaved population, and it is good to learn that a Coloured man, Mr. John Edward Richards, aged 25, became a catechist on estates in St. Peter.[54]

In setting the ministry of the Church on a firm footing, Bishop Coleridge gave due consideration to the financial support of the clergy and catechists. In fact, very early after his appointment and consecration he raised with His Majesty's Treasury the question of clergy salaries, especially as there was likely to be some delay in payments reaching the West Indies. He was informed that the Treasury would honour Bills drawn quarterly by him in his Diocese for any salaries that were due, and his clergy should be directed to draw such quarterly Bills upon the Board of Treasury for their stipends, provided that the Bills were countersigned by the Bishop.[55] It had also been enacted that a sum not exceeding £6,300 per annum would be voted to the Dioceses of Jamaica and Barbados and the Leeward Islands, as from 5 April 1824, to pay the salaries of ministers, catechists and schoolmasters. Of this amount, a sum not exceeding £2,100 would be granted annually to the Diocese of Jamaica and the Diocese of Barbados and the Leeward Islands would annually receive a sum not exceeding £4,200. The Act had also set the annual salary of a minister at £300 currency.[56]

Very early in his episcopate, however, the Bishop appealed to the local Legislature for more funds to increase the salary of the parochial clergy from £300 to £500 currency and, from a statement in his petition to Parliament for funds towards the erection of St. Mary's Chapel, this request seems to have been met.[57] In 1830 the Bishop publicly rejoiced that, thanks to the liberality of the local Legislature, the income of the parochial clergy was commensurate with their needs and status in society.[58] With an annual salary of £500, a rent-free parsonage (maintained by the parish), or an allowance for one, a portion of glebe, and various fees connected with his pastoral duties, a Rector was indeed in a good financial position.[59]

With regard to certain assistant clergy, for example the Rev. W.M. Harte and the Rev. C.C. Cummins who became curates of St. Michael's and ministers of the 'District' (St. Mary's) respectively, the salary was £75 sterling per quarter (£450 currency per annum). Other assistant curates received the equivalent of £150 currency per annum. There is evidence, however, that in some cases assistant curates got more than this, while others got considerably less. For example, the Rev. G.P. Culpepper (at the Cathedral) received £225 currency per annum, while the Rev. J.K. West, BA, and the Rev. E. Lovell, MA (both at St. George) received £75 each per annum.[60]

Provision was also made for the catechists, whose quarterly salaries ranged from £10 to £25 currency.[61] There was no uniformity in payment of catechists, for some served as teachers in schools, for which they were also remunerated as we shall see in the next chapter. It is interesting to note that some teacher-catechists received part of their salaries from the Bishop's funds, as was the case of Mr. Nathaniel Fitzpatrick in the parish of Christ Church.[62]

That the salaries for clergy and catechists were set on a relatively sound footing was due to the support the Bishop received from His Majesty's Government, the local Legislature, the SPG, the SPCK and the 'Mixed Fund'. In 1838 it was stated that the mother country was responsible for the salaries of the Bishop, the Archdeacon, nine Assistant Curates and the Garrison Chaplain; the colonial Legislature was responsible for the eleven rectors and three and a half Assistant Curates ('half' represents shared responsibility, not 50 per cent of salary). The Codrington Trust Estates were responsible for three-and-a-half staff at Codrington College and Codrington School.[63]

Closely related to the provision of salaries were the arrangements for leave of absence. In 1829 a circular was sent from His Majesty's Government to the Bishops of Jamaica and Barbados and the Leeward Islands, informing them that leave of absence to officers of the Civil Service could not be granted for a period exceeding six months, and the same should be prescribed for all 'Ecclesiastical functionaries' within their respective dioceses.[64] In answer to a request for leave for a 'Stipendiary Clergyman' of the Diocese of Jamaica, Bishop Lipscomb was informed that the clergyman should be paid a half of his salary for the period, and this ruling should be conveyed to all clergy for their information.[65] In cases of leave of absence for clergy whose emoluments exceeded £600 per annum, such clergy should be liable to deduction of a 'moiety' when absent from duties for private purposes.[66]

Bishop Coleridge's policy on leave of absence for clergy reflected the stipulations of the British government. He declared that if sufficient reason was given by a clergyman and adequate arrangements were made for the care of souls in the parish, a leave of six months 'from the time of embarkation, exclusive of the passage to and from the Mother Country', would be granted.[67]

Bishop Coleridge also considered provision for the widows and children of deceased clergy, and so 'The Society for the Relief of the Widows and Fatherless Children of Clergymen in the Diocese of Barbados and the Leeward Islands' was founded in 1838 with the Bishop as President. The Board of Management comprised the Bishop, the archdeacons and rural deans and some members of the clergy. The joint-treasurers were the Hon. R. Bowcher Clarke and the Rev. R.F. King, and the secretary was the Rev. T.F.

Barrow. A local Board was also formed in each Rural Deanery, but all subscriptions and all recommended applications were to be forwarded to the General Board, of which five members would constitute a quorum. The General Board would also fix the amount of relief to be granted to distressed widows and orphans. It was agreed that a sum, not exceeding £100 sterling, should be at the annual disposal of the General Board. Relief would be granted only to these cases of distress: widows whose annual income was not £60 sterling, and those children who did not have £15 sterling a year either in their own right or through their mother's income.

The widow would receive £60 sterling a year if she was not receiving relief for children. A boy would be granted £30 sterling a year until he reached the age of eighteen, but if he was being educated for the ministry then relief would be continued until he was twenty-three. In the case of a girl, relief would be granted until she was twenty-one. If she got married before this age, she would not receive relief. Also, no relief would be granted to a widow who re-married. To ensure these provisions for his family a clergyman of the Diocese had to pay £16 for the first year, and a subsequent annual subscription of £8 for five consecutive years. For a further five years he would subscribe £6 annually, after which period his annual subscription would become £4. The scheme met with the full support of the clergy and by 11 January 1839 £700 had been subscribed, with some arrears still due, and the bank deposit stood at £696.[68]

Bishop Coleridge demonstrated immense ability in establishing the administrative machinery and in recruiting, training, and deploying his clergy to meet the great challenges, particularly of the amelioration of the labouring classes. His determined policy was shown in his support of the Rev. William Harte. His institution of the ministries of readers and catechists as 'auxiliaries' to the parochial clergy did much to extend the Church's pastoral care of the enslaved population on the plantations in Barbados. The Bishop's efforts to make adequate financial provision for his clergy, as well as for their families at their decease, must have been a source of much encouragement to them. It is pleasing to note that one of his local recruits became a Rector in Barbados. Other Barbadian graduates went forth to serve in various parts of the Diocese.

Coleridge's success in organising Codrington College as both a centre of higher education and also of theological studies evidently attracted the attention of his brother Bishop in Jamaica. It is interesting to note that in 1839 the Island Council of Jamaica requested that Bishop Coleridge send them copies of the Statutes, Bye Laws, Foundation Charter and regulations for the government of Codrington College, as well as any other papers relative to the internal management of that institution, its patrons and its Association with the SPG.[69] In a letter to the Rev. John Keble in 1834 Bishop Coleridge had expressed the hope that, with the prospect of a regular steamship between Jamaica and the Leeward Islands, the benefits of Codrington College would be offered to that island.[70] However, the Diocese of Jamaica was to go its own way in theological education and establish its own theological college (St. Peter's) in 1883.

# 5

# PUBLIC EDUCATION
## INTEGRAL TO AMELIORATION AND EVANGELISATION

FROM BISHOP COLERIDGE'S 'NOTEBOOK' we receive a picture of the general condition of education in Barbados at the beginning of his episcopate. There was provision for the education of poor White children in every parish, while for the Coloureds and Black there was only one school, situated near the Old Church Yard in St. Michael. These schools for the poor Whites were scattered and lacked administrative co-ordination.

The schools in St. Andrew were in 'improper' hands. There was once a 'good' school in Christ Church, but it was closed for lack of funds. One school in St. Lucy was at a low ebb, and there were other schools dispersed about the parish. One small school could be found in St. Philip. In St. John there were scattered schools, and a Sunday School with seventy children 'neatly dressed' and 'breakfasted' by the Rector on Sundays at his own expense. In St. George was located a boarding school for girls, and in St. James and St. Thomas there was a sprinkling of schools, as was the case in St. Peter and in St. Joseph. The situation in St. Michael was more promising, as we shall see later. As for the curriculum of these schools, there was very defective instruction in English grammar, writing and arithmetic, and no attention was paid to religion, much to the distress of the Bishop.[1]

The Bishop disclosed that his policy would be to establish in each parish a 'district school' for the education of White boys and girls, not only in religion but also in writing, arithmetic and English grammar, in short, as he put it, 'in whatever will breed up a race of good book-keepers and managers of Estates – men of good principles, well-disciplined, well-informed, and who may become from inclination, qualification and opportunity good instructors of the Blacks of the respective estates'. Such a school would be administered according to the same system as obtained at the Central School in Bridgetown.[2]

The Central School had been established in St. Michael in 1819 for the board, clothing and education of poor White children. The Governor, Lord Combermere, had given much support to this project and had laid the foundation stone of the building. The Legislature also had demonstrated their generous support by a grant of £800 currency. By 1825 three children from each parish were being admitted to the school, and as many more as the building could accommodate, with the fees of £25 currency paid each child by the respective parish.

There were about sixty-five boarders (boys only), as well as day-scholars. Girls were educated during the day in reading, arithmetic and needlework. The head of the school was a clergyman, the Rev. John Packer, whose mother and aunt managed the house and supervised the girls at needlework. A committee of clergy and leading gentry governed the school, which was incorporated by an Act of the local Legislature. In the Bishop's view, the school was well administered and it reflected 'great credit on the Island'.[3] The founding of this school, later called Combermere as a tribute to Lord Combermere, was interpreted as a fulfilment of the intention of the late Colonel Henry Drax, a great pioneer in the sugar industry in Barbados, who had bequeathed £2,000 for the establishment of a school in Bridgetown.[4]

In St. Michael there was also a grammar school near the Parish Church, for the education of the 'better sort'. The students were instructed in Greek and Latin; the Master was 'ignorant' of the former and 'deficient' in the latter. The Bishop had visited the school with his chaplains and encouraged the boys to be diligent. He had also lent the Head Master and Head Boy ('a promising lad') many books from his own library. He expressed his desire to place the school on a better foundation by examining more closely the will of the Founder.[5]

This school, known as Harrison's Free School, was founded by Thomas

Harrison, a merchant in Bridgetown, who had purchased land near St. Michael's Church and it was conveyed by deed on 30 July 1733.[6] The Bishop further expressed his desire to examine the application of funds, the course of studies and the qualifications of the Master. As he saw it, the grammar school should be the nursery for 'my' college (Codrington College), and should attract children of the 'better sort' in Bridgetown and from other parts of the island, who would receive a liberal education. The Bishop himself would keep a close eye on the school.[7]

The Bishop proposed a bill for the Legislature to place at the disposal of the committee of the Central School the surplus of all monies remaining after the annual current expenses of the institution, but which was tied up by an Act of Incorporation. He sought to use such monies to erect a separate building, detached from, yet near, the building for boys, for the board, clothing and education of White girls, thus extending equal advantage to both sexes.[8] By 1828 the Bishop could report favourably on the Harrison's Free School and two Central Schools for boys and girls respectively in St. Michael.[9]

The Bishop's policy concerning the education of poor Whites was to centralise it in each parish. For example, he proposed to consolidate the existing parochial payments for scattered schools in St. John into one fund and establish a day-school for White boys and girls on the vacant green in front of the church, near the parsonage. He suggested that in addition to the existing sum of £300 paid by the parishes to cover the three areas in which the schools functioned, a few more hundred pounds would support the proposed school. The Bishop also noted that the Rector and General Haynes were very much in favour of his proposal, and that the parish was wealthy.[10]

The Bishop's policy was further demonstrated by his instruction to the Rector of St. Andrew that he should look into the funds of the school in that parish (which stood at £80 currency, plus £20 with house and five acres, and probably other bequests), with a view to erecting a Central School for the whole parish.[11] Very gratifying to the Bishop was the opening of the Central District School in St. Peter. All annual payments had been transferred to it, and the children were provided with daily 'dinner', as they came to school in the morning and returned home at night.[12]

There is an interesting account of the consolidation of education for poor White children in St. Peter. Initially the children were placed in the hands of a variety of teachers, chosen generally by parents and receiving a small sum from the Vestry. The Bishop soon found it difficult to ascertain the qualifications of the teachers, and in 1826 the school was abandoned. The sixteen remaining children were placed under a Master, who received £60 per annum, with an allowance for meals. In 1827 the Rector, the Rev. W.P. Hinds, made an appeal among his wealthy parishioners, who responded most generously, and a school was opened in the same year. In 1828 it was reported that the children had made much progress in reading and writing, and their 'cyphering' was remarkable. Also, they were punctual in their attendance, well-mannered and most appreciative, and it was hoped that they would be useful members of society and take their places with credit. It was noted that there was an increase in the number of children admitted to the school; the boarding establishment was extended, and the Committee of Management was compelled to increase expenses to the sum of £400.[13]

It is clear that the Bishop's policy was to centralise education for the children of poor Whites in the various parishes. These latter, he thought, were in a deplorable state of 'ignorance, pride, and vice'. He observed that, despite their 'low birth and morals', the poor Whites prided themselves on their colour and considered themselves on the same social level as the 'first families' of White people of the island. To him they appeared too proud to work and required, more than did the Blacks, the ameliorating influence of education. He stated that both in sermons and in conversations he had called the attention of the 'higher whites' to the sad state of these people. It was not only a matter of sound religious principle, he maintained, but also a matter of sound policy that they be educated, for if they were left behind the Blacks in education, the consequences were obvious.[14]

With regard to the 'higher whites', the Bishop held the view that their education should be in the hands of the clergy who, he argued, had the appropriate educational qualifications, having been properly trained and having assented to the Thirty-Nine Articles. He also considered that the clergy were of high moral character, that they knew how to submit to legitimate authority and would forge a good link with the influential parishioners, whose children they were already educating.[15]

We have noted earlier that the only school for the Coloureds which the

Bishop found in existence on his arrival, was that near the Old Church Yard in St. Michael. This school had been started in 1818 by one Lieutenant Luggar, who received £100 sterling from the Church Missionary Society (CMS) for the Master. There was a large school-room for about four hundred children, boys and girls in the same room. It operated on the same national system of education as did the Central School, and books listed in the SPCK catalogue were used. The Bishop took in hand the management of this school, and assumed sole responsibility for the payment of the Master in order to obviate irregularities which, he thought, might creep in. He was determined that this 'powerful' school should not get out of hand.[16]

Bishop Coleridge proceeded with his programme of providing education for the Coloureds. From his own account we learn that in Roebuck and the Bay, two of the 'most populous and demoralised quarters' of Bridgetown, schools had been started with White masters and mistresses. There were 250 children being instructed in reading and religious duties, the girls (about 100) being instructed in needlework also. The schools, known as Charity Schools, were open to all Coloured children, free or enslaved, the latter being required to produce a letter of permission from their owners. The schools, their masters and mistresses, were under the supervision of the Rev. John Packer, 'that valuable Master of the Central School' in the Bishop's judgement. He was appointed by the Bishop himself to visit each school once a week and make sure that the same system was pursued as at the Central School.[17] Again, we see the Bishop's desire to have the curriculum and administration of a school for Coloureds modelled on those of a school for Whites, he himself keeping the reins of control in his own hands through the oversight of his 'trusted man', John Packer.

The Bishop disclosed that he had arranged to open another school for Coloured children near his own residence. This school would be under a White Master and under the supervision of the trusted John Packer. The area surrounding 'Gibraltar' was thickly populated, and the Bishop thought that the distance from there to the town was too far for the children. In his zeal to start this school, he apportioned part of £3,900 sterling annually allotted to the clergy and catechists in the diocese.[18] There was no doubt that he was enthusiastic about providing education for the Coloureds, but he was equally enthusiastic that the 'right' teaching and supervision be established.

His Lordship clearly did not believe in a system of co-education. His policy of separating girls from boys was adopted equally in the Central School and in the School for Coloureds in the Old Church Yard. Since the Master of this latter school received the 'handsome' salary of £100, and the Matron £25, the Bishop suggested that the wife of the Master should look after the girls in order to justify her husband's salary. The Bishop accepted the office of president of this school and suggested that the President of the island be its Patron. The Bishop also expressed his intention to preach at the school, as he did at the Central School, in order to demonstrate that he was equally disposed to the 'spiritual improvement' of all classes. He was careful to make the distinction between the 'spiritual' and the 'civil'. His task, as he saw it, was to teach all to read and understand the Bible for their salvation and for the performance of the several duties in their 'respective stations'.[19]

A school for the children of indigent persons of colour and enslaved was opened in Hole Town, St. James. There were forty-four children in attendance. Another such school was opened near Oistins in Christ Church, with a roll of forty-nine. Two were opened in Bridgetown, one with thirty-two boys and the other with forty-three girls.[20] A request for a school from the coloured population of Speight's Town was received by the Bishop through their Rector. An encouraging reply was forthcoming, accompanied by a donation of £10 from his personal funds.[21]

For his entire education programme, the Bishop received invaluable assistance from the SPCK. It was fortunate for him that Lord Combermere had already given a lead in corresponding with the SPCK, with the result that in 1820 the first District Committee of the SPCK in Barbados had been formed in connection with support for Central Schools. Through this committee tracts of the Society were conveyed in large numbers, either by donation or by purchase, to schools and to the general public.[22] In 1825 Bishop Coleridge changed the title of the committee to the 'Diocesan Committee'. In 1827 there was a further development when he established two groups: 'The Barbados Society for the Education of the Poor', devoted to the Central Schools, and 'The Diocesan Committee', promote Christian knowledge throughout the island and indeed throughout the Diocese.[23] About this time there also came into existence the Ladies Branch Association for the Education of Female Children of the Coloured Poor in the Principles of the

Established Church of England', and we shall later see what active support they gave to this cause.

Bishop Coleridge, like Bishop Lipscomb of Jamaica, initially received £500 from the SPCK to assist him in inaugurating his educational programme. The SPCK also undertook to print editions of the National School Books, at the request of the Bishop. In 1826 it was reported that an 'ample supply' of books had been forwarded,[24] and in 1828 it was stated that the cost of books ordered, received and distributed by sale to the Coloured poor had amounted to £577.12s.7d.[25] It was further reported that two colonial schools for Coloured children had been established in 1827, accommodating 430 free Coloured and 454 enslaved people, and that some of the best scholars in the schools for Coloured were employed as teachers of reading. Also, two more colonial schools were opened by the Bishop, with his expressed intention to 'convert and civilise' the West Indian enslaved people.[26] By 1829 the schools in Bridgetown for Coloured children were accommodating 352: 106 free boys, 61 free girls, 102 enslaved boys and 83 enslaved girls.[27]

The SPCK was indeed one of the principal sources of support for the Bishop's programme of providing education for Coloured and enslaved children. The Diocesan Committee had become an effective medium of communication between the island and the 'Venerable Society in England'. Bibles, prayer books, homilies, tracts, and National School Books, all on the list of the Society, were received and distributed at cost price (a 'very low one'), but considerable social benefit to the committee. Some books were also received gratuitously. With regard to direct financial support, the SPCK was generous. In addition to other grants, in 1832 they contributed substantially – like the SPG – to the rebuilding of chapels and schools destroyed by the hurricane of 1831. The sum was £2,000 sterling.

In the period of Apprenticeship the Diocese was to benefit again from the SPCK, by a grant of £10,000 in 1834 to the West Indian dioceses for the erection of schools and places of worship. Between 1825 and 1837 the Diocese of Barbados and the Leeward Islands received support from the SPCK amounting to a total of £15,000 sterling.[28]

Active support for the education of the poor Coloured was also given by the 'Ladies Branch Association for the Education of Female Children of the Coloured Poor in the Principles of the Established Church of England'.

In 1828 they reported on a school in Barbados for 144 girls (of whom 61 were free and 83 enslaved), who were taught reading, writing, needlework and also religious instruction. The Association was clearly receiving good support from the public, as the statement of accounts showed: 'Income £173.10s.4¼d. Expenditure £171.10s.8¾d.'[29] As R.H. Schomburgk records, this Association continued to make a worthwhile contribution to the education of the poorer classes.[30]

To increase the educational outreach to the labouring class, the Bishop promoted the establishment of Sunday Schools to instruct the enslaved people on the estates. By 1827 Sunday Schools were started in many places.[31] The Bishop felt that the ability to read was of basic importance for the advancement of religion, so this was the initial thrust of the instruction given.[32] By 1829 there was a Sunday School in each parish. Lessons were provided on Sundays, as well as worship and a lecture on a religious subject. Daily reading was also encouraged on each estate (in private schools, at which we shall look later). In this whole endeavour the Bishop was careful to get the consent of proprietors.[33] He saw the importance of Sunday Schools in enabling the enslaved adults to read for themselves the 'charter of their salvation', and in preparing the young for the 'Apostolic rite of Confirmation'.[34]

The establishment of estate schools was another of the Bishop's innovations in the education of enslaved people. It was his wish that a daily school be established on every estate for the education of the young. Such a school, he thought, should be subject to periodical inspection by the parochial clergyman, and be placed under the care of a White tenant or servant, or, in cases where these were not available, under some 'respectable person of colour who can read'. The Bishop commended the model on the SPG's Codrington Trust Estates. The estate school, he argued, would help children to read, and the clergyman would find his flock on Sundays zealous for instruction and dependent upon him. The Bishop exhorted the clergy to pay due respect to the proprietors, whose co-operation was absolutely necessary for the success of this educational provision. As he said, 'If planter cannot trust minister, whom will he trust?'[35]

In 1830 the Bishop gave his summary of the state of education at that stage. The parochial schools were now consolidated; new schools, organised along the lines of the National System of education, were established in the 'chief towns and small villages' of every colony (his summary included other parts of his diocese); there were private schools on estates for the daily instruction of Black children in reading and in the catechism; Sunday Schools were thriving and some 'local' teachers were using their own homes, after working hours, as places of education, with the result that a good number of the enslaved adult population were being taught to read and understand the Scriptures.[36]

The Bishop also commented on the large and regular attendances at school, which demonstrated the progress in education, not only by the establishment of schools both in towns and villages, but also by better organisation of existing schools. He stressed that both parent and master should be brought to see the importance of each child learning to read. He also urged that care should be taken to 'inculcate first principles on which education rests its claims' lest authorities of parochial schools, through 'misplaced economy or want of vacancies for fresh children', should send into the world children with 'undisciplined tempers or without sufficient religious principle to influence conduct'.[37] The civilising role of education and religious instruction was clearly uppermost in the Bishop's mind.

During the period of Apprenticeship Bishop Coleridge worked hard to implement his programme of education for the Blacks. He stuck to the model of Black education which existed on the Codrington Estates. He sought direct support from the British government for his programme and was informed by Lord Glenelg, the Secretary of State for the Colonies, that requests for assistance should be sent to him.[38] Lord Glenelg later sent word that steps were being taken concerning Black education in pursuance of a Resolution which had been passed by both Houses of Parliament in June 1833. Lord Glenelg also mentioned that the House of Commons had shown marked enthusiasm and had voted a grant of £25,000 for the education of the recently emancipated population in the West Indies. As he put it, they were 'disposed liberally to contribute towards the promotion of the Education of that large class of community, on whose religious and moral improvement the final success of the great measure of emancipation, under Providence, mainly depends'.

Lord Glenelg went on to cite the interest of the proprietors in Barbados in Black education, particularly in diffusing among the labouring class 'those principles which afford the best security for good order, and the right discharge of every social duty'. He commended the generosity of individuals in Barbados, but thought that in a matter of such magnitude the Legislature should follow the example of the British government with regard to the maintenance of 'liberal and comprehensive principles' of schools for the education of emancipated Blacks in Barbados.[39]

Lord Glenelg had already given instructions that the Lords Commissioners of His Majesty's Treasury be informed of Bishop Coleridge's measures, for adoption by the government in accordance with part of the Fifth Resolution on the matter of Colonial Slavery, dated 12 June 1833; that the government be enabled to defray expenses incurred in aiding local legislatures in providing liberal and comprehensive principles for the religious and moral education of the Black population which would be emancipated; that replies to inquiries sent out to various Societies in England concerning the means of educating Blacks were received and placed in the hands of Rev. John Sterling, a man well versed in matters related to the Black population and whose report had been submitted.[40]

In his report Sterling called for an immediate and sustained educational programme among the freed people. He pointed out the shortcomings of the existing religious education and expressed doubts about the efficacy of the existing teachers and methods in making an impact on poor Black children. He advocated that the whole matter should be placed in the hands of religious bodies, the Catholics being treated as a special case. He suggested that rules be formulated to make the system efficient; secondary education should be for all classes; and teacher-training was necessary for the transformation of education in the West Indies.[41] Bishop Coleridge's suggestion, that Black education be placed in the hands of the religious bodies which were already active in the West Indian colonies, had won the day.[42]

Lord Glenelg further proposed small disbursements of funds for erecting schools such as obtained in England. For the erection of new schools in Colonies and Settlements – to which the Act for the Abolition of Slavery applied – he would recommend to the Lords Commissioners, as a first step, a sum not exceeding £20,000. For the new schools he recommended that inspectors be employed to report on them. In order that competent teachers be supplied, he also recommended that two National Schools be established, one in the West Indies and one in Mauritius. Bishop Coleridge hoped that buildings would be hired or purchased immediately for the inauguration of these schools, which would admit pupils recommended by the respective Societies or their agents in the colonies. The children, it was felt, would have already received a certain amount of elementary education and in a short period would be instructed in the art of teaching. The masters and mistresses of the schools should have high qualifications and be of sound character.

In addition to the sum of £20,000 already recommended for the erection of new schools, Glenelg recommended £5,000 per annum to defray the expenses of the proposed National School. The local legislatures should provide a portion of the annual expenditure for the maintenance of schools for Black education.[43] It was later mentioned that Bishop Coleridge was prepared to receive applications from those Societies which would assist towards the erection of school houses for Black education.[44]

Lord Glenelg laid down the terms and conditions of application for Parliamentary Grants towards the erection of schools for Black education. No portion of the funds appropriated to Black education could be withdrawn by any Society. The school which was to be aided should conform to the principles and plan of the sponsoring Society. A statement on the colony and situation of the school to be erected should accompany the application, as well as the number of scholars anticipated, the estimated cost of the erection and any other particulars that would show that the proposed school would be used exclusively for the education of Blacks. Each Society was to give a firm guarantee that a portion of the estimated cost of each school would come from its own funds. Lord Glenelg further mentioned that it would be helpful to know how many schools each Society hoped to erect, the estimated cost and the amount the Society would contribute. He also disclosed that all schools built with government funds would be subject to inspection by an officer appointed by His Majesty's Government. However, there was no intention on the part of government to interfere with religious education in schools, but only 'to assert that they really conduce to the moral and religious education and improvement of the Black population, and thus answer the end for which public money has been advanced'.[45]

Replies to the Bishop's Circular to the Clergy in 1835 give us some indication of the state of education at this time. The Rev. W.M. Jackson, Curate of St. Lucy, stated that there were some unordained teachers under the supervision of the clergy: Edward J. Archer, aged 30, a parochial school master, a communicant not assisted by his wife, was paid £66.13.4 per annum by the Vestry; John Barrow, aged 36, communicant, who had a flourishing day-school and assisted with the adult Sunday School, was aided by his wife, in the capacity of an unpaid volunteer. In all, there were some 700 adults and 500 children under direct instruction of clergymen and school teachers in St. Lucy.[46]

From the Rector of Christ Church, Rev. C.C. Gill, came the report that there were 5 School Masters (3 Catechists, 1 Sunday School Master, 1 School Master). The Master of the Parochial Boys' School, Mr. Nathaniel Fitzpatrick, and his wife (Mistress of the Parochial Girls' School) received £150 jointly. For his duties as Catechist Mr. Fitzpatrick received no additional remuneration; in any case part of his salary was met from the Bishop's funds.[47]

The Rev. W.D. Sealy, Rector of St. Peter's, reported that he was assisted by 2 School Masters and 1 Catechist. Mr. Stoute, a White man, was in charge of White or parochial schools, and his wife was in charge of the girls. They received £80 jointly from the Vestry. There was a school house on the glebe. Mr. Massiah, a Black man, aged 34, was in charge of St. Peter's Benevolent School and his wife, a Black woman, was in charge of the girls' needlework. They received £50 jointly from the Bishop. There were also 16 private schools in the parish for charity children.[48]

The Bishop must have been happy with the results of a survey done by his Archdeacon, Thomas Parry, of the schools established between 1825 and 1834 for providing education for the poorer classes in Barbados: 27 National Schools with an aggregate attendance of 1,574; 3 Infant Schools with 261; 14 Evening Schools with 834; 92 Estate Schools with 3,075 and 19 Sunday Schools with 1,679, giving a total of 155 schools with an aggregate attendance of 7,447.[49] Another statement in 1834 showed that there were National Schools in all parishes, as well as Sunday Schools in all parish churches, chapels of ease, and chapel schools (at which there were also National Schools). It was also stated that 2,315 persons were receiving instruction for baptism.[50] With his encouragement of the clergy and the 'auxiliaries' (the readers and catechists) much fruit had been borne, and the Bishop could be pleased with the progress made.

From a list of the salaries for the quarter ending 6 July 1839, we get some information concerning the annual scale of salaries for teachers, readers, and catechists in the National, Estate and Sunday Schools: 32 teachers received from the Mixed Fund between £20 and £50 each, the majority receiving £30 each; readers and catechists received £100 from His Majesty's Treasury, as did Mr. Morle, while Mr. C.A. Newsam (later a student of Codrington College and then Assistant Curate of St. Andrew) received £100 from SPG; 7 male teachers received £25 each and I female £15 from the Christian Faith Society. The total expenditure for that year (calculated on the basis of the quarter) was:

Mixed Fund: £2,887
HM Treasury: £700
SPG: £390
SPCK: £105
Christian Faith Society: £700
Total: £4,782 sterling[51]

It is clear that Bishop Coleridge had won the confidence of both His Majesty's Government and the missionary societies in his tremendous programme of establishing primary education, particularly among the Black population. The Moravians and Methodists, who had also been active in public education among the Black, benefited from the Negro Education Grant and were able to establish four schools each.[52]

Bishop Coleridge not only laid the foundations, in large measure, for primary education in Barbados; he also laid them for the development of secondary and tertiary education. Harrison's Free School and the Central Schools in Bridgetown, developed during his episcopate, were to expand further and to become Harrison College, Combermere School and Queen's College respectively. In St. John, the Codrington Grammar School, relocated at the Chaplain's Lodge on the Codrington Estates, was to become The Lodge School. The re-organisation of Codrington College introduced collegiate education not only in theology, but also in classics, logic, mathematics, and some subjects in science and medicine.[53] The College henceforth was an institution of higher learning, providing its own Testamurs, 'SCC' and 'ThSCC', which were equivalent to Arts degrees in Classics and Mathematics, and Divinity respectively.[54]

In 1875 the College became the first University College in the West Indies when it was affiliated to the University of Durham, England, and successive generations of scholars were to receive degrees in Classics, Mathematics and Theology and Licences in Theology of Durham University through their studies at the College. Since 1965 the College has enjoyed another affiliation, that with the University of the West Indies (UWI). Students now read for degrees and licences in Theology granted by UWI.

Thus the labours of Bishop Coleridge have had far-reaching consequences for primary, secondary and tertiary education in Barbados. It is true that in his educational policy he conformed to the class and gender stratification of his day. But there is no gainsaying the fact that the provision of education, particularly for the Blacks both in the pre-Emancipation and Apprenticeship periods, was due mainly to his zeal, and to his conviction that education was vital to amelioration and evangelisation.

*St. John's Church*

*St. Luke's Chapel*

*Society Chapel*

*All Saint Chapel*

*St. Marks*

*All Saint Chapel*

*Society Chapel*

*St. Mark's Chapel*

*Society Chapel*

*All Saint Chapel*

*Trinity Chapel*

*Lawrence Chapel School*

# 6

# PASTORAL CARE AND AFRICAN CUSTOMS

IN PASTORAL CARE, as in public education, Bishop Coleridge was concerned for all classes of Barbadian society, and this meant encouraging the clergy to win the confidence of White parishioners and proprietors by their deportment and disposition, while involving themselves particularly in the circumstances of the enslaved population. He gave guidance to his clergy in such aspects of pastoral care as the oversight and visitation of schools, visiting, generally, and preaching; baptism, Holy Communion and marriage; and burial of the dead. Sunday markets and dances, the cult of obeah, superstition, polygamy and concubinage were Black customs and practices against which, the Bishop thought, the Church's pastoral care should be directed. He encouraged the clergy themselves to set an example of zeal, discipline and studiousness, and win the respect of all, as the Established Clergy.

Bishop Coleridge indeed had a 'high' view of ordination and of the ministry of the Church of England. For him there was a clear distinction between the unordained and the ordained. The layman might be pious, learned and apt to teach, but he was not a minister until he was ordained by the hands of a Bishop. This was entirely different from the practice of the 'Scottish Presbyterians' and 'Continental Protestants' who, in the Bishop's view, had deviated from the 'ancient line of Episcopacy'. He maintained that bishops and their 'co-adjutors' – priests and deacons – were duly ordained in an uninterrupted succession from the Apostles, and that the 'English Church' had retained the symbols of faith – Scriptures, Lord's Prayer, Ten Commandments, Ancient Creeds and Sacraments ordained by Christ. He argued that, at the Reformation, there was 'no violent disruption from the doctrine and discipline of the Catholic or Universal Church; we did not deny the Episcopacy of Rome; but only its Papal and Tridentine assumptions'.

In his opinion, also, the line of bishops continued through Thomas Cranmer to the present Archbishop, and so ordination in the Church of England stood in succession to the earliest of Christ's Ministers.[1] Bishop Coleridge again and again emphasised the doctrine of Apostolic Succession and the importance of Episcopacy for guaranteeing the validity of ordination and the unity of the Church. For him there was nothing 'more momentous or alarming than the exercise of that power of Ordination, which the great Head of the Church has delegated and entrusted to the highest order of His Ministers'.[2] Also, he maintained that the essential characteristic of the Christian Ministry was 'unity of purpose', and that the essence of Episcopacy was 'unity of action'.[3]

Bishop Coleridge's views clearly reflected those of the contemporary Oxford Movement of which his friend John Keble was one of the leading lights. However much he admired the labours of the ministers of the Moravian and Methodist Churches and of the Scottish Kirk, which had led to conversion and enlightenment, he still felt that they lacked the 'moral weight of the Established Clergy'.[4] He regretted that societies were encouraged, institutions formed, vows taken, and new doctrines and practices introduced, without regard for the 'episcopal pre-eminence'.[5] He therefore exhorted his clergy to be diligent in the study of the Scriptures, the Latin and Greek Fathers, the theological works of the seventeenth-century Anglican Divines and the Thirty-Nine Articles, and to be faithful to the Rubrics and Liturgy of the Church of England. He also encouraged them to use the Clerical Library, to which every clergyman had access.[7]

The SPCK had assisted the Bishop with the establishment of several clerical libraries in the Diocese. Dr. Thomas Bray, the founder of the SPCK, had been concerned for the theological education of the clergy overseas, and so the Bishop expressed his gratitude to 'Dr. Bray's Associates' for providing copies of the Family Bible and a complete set of the Society's books and tracts at a 'low price'.[8] With such a provision of literature the Bishop impressed upon his clergy that they should equip themselves for the more effective exercise of their ministry. He admonished them that they should be on their guard against the liberal attitude of 'individuals of every varying shade of religious opinion', which constituted a real danger to religion.[9] There is no doubt that Bishop Coleridge's view of Episcopacy, as essential to the unity of the Church and the validity of Orders, determined his attitude to other religious bodies and his contention that pastoral care could be properly provided only by the Established Clergy.

As we have seen in the previous chapter, Bishop Coleridge saw education as integral to amelioration and evangelisation. He therefore considered it of utmost importance that the clergy should involve themselves in the life and work of schools in their respective parishes. He declared that every day a clergyman spent in a parochial school would be a day gained in his 'after ministry'. Such a school, he thought, should be among the 'most cherished objects of ministerial care'. In his opinion, the clergyman in reaching the child would reach the parent, and so reach his neighbour; the child would respect the clergyman, and the parent would love the clergyman for caring for his child.[10] The clergyman should show no less diligence in his superintendence of daily schools on the estates, with the co-operation of proprietors, for on Sundays he would have a flock more desirous of instruction.[11]

The Bishop was in no doubt that the very success of a clergyman's ministry depended on his attention to the schools in his parish in which the young and old, infant and adult, should equally be taught to read and understand the Scriptures. As he put it, 'catechising is with you the very fulfilment of your ministry'.[12] The Bishop thought that religious instruction would ensure the moral thrust of education and eradicate such vices as 'profligacy, theft and robbery'. He therefore exhorted the clergy to be everywhere – in Church on Sunday, and during the week in schools, on plantations and in dwellings of the flock – always moving about, 'ready to teach, explain and admonish'.[13]

In advocating the provision of a daily meal and uniforms for children, Bishop Coleridge showed another aspect of his care for children. He argued that a simple meal could be provided for sixty or seventy children at no great expense. He stated that, in efforts to improve the child's heart, mind and conduct by daily instruction, the child's body should not be neglected.

Also, the provision of a 'neat, but plain dress' would help the child to appreciate a respectable appearance which would serve him in good stead when he was called in later life to a situation of 'trust and authority' on the plantation or to some useful employment generally in society.' Bishop Coleridge was thus concerned that care should be taken of the total person, with due consideration for his social improvement. The formation of a Daily Meal Society was due to the Bishop's leadership and pastoral care.[15]

The necessity of visiting was considered by Bishop Coleridge as an essential aspect of pastoral care. He encouraged the clergy to visit all classes, and he was particularly concerned that there be a free and easy intercourse between them and their 'slave parishioners of all ages'. As he saw it, there was the need for a 'spiritual pastor' who would cope with the difficulties and stresses of parishioners and give them instruction and guidance when they were sick in estate hospitals or in their cottages, as well as encouragement when they were in good health. He encouraged the clergy to visit at the times allowed by proprietors and at the convenience of the Blacks.

When the clergy visited them, they should call at the 'gate of their little garden' or at the 'door of their lowly dwelling', and inquire after their 'temporal and spiritual welfare'. If a clergyman found that an estate was too populous, or that the distance between estates prevented him from visiting frequently, then he should encourage the Blacks to come to his own house after working hours or on Sunday evenings, with the permission of the respective proprietors. The Bishop did not anticipate that a proprietor would object to the 'freest intercourse between people and their lawful spiritual adviser'. The clergyman, on his part, should time his visits wisely, and 'pay to the Manager every proper civility on your way to the dwellings of his people'. In order that a 'plea to visit the Minister' might not be a pretext to escape from work, the clergyman should refuse to see a Black who did not receive permission from the Manager.[16]

Bishop Coleridge felt that in mixing with all classes of people the clergy could speak 'a word in season' that might check vice and encourage virtue. Also, the clergy would get first-hand knowledge of the 'temporal wants' of their parishioners. If the clergy themselves could not relieve these needs because of their 'slender resources', they should bring them to the attention of the more wealthy parishioners, and this might be 'a means of rescuing a family from penury and distress'.[17] With regard to the sick, the clergy should be particularly sensitive and sympathetic. The Bishop encouraged them to console the sick by use of the Scriptures, and he exhorted them to use the tract, 'On Visiting the Sick', at the end of the *Clergyman's Instructor*, which they should have always in their hands. This tract provided suitable devotions and passages of Scripture. The clergy should respond to a call from the sick without delay; they should not make their visits too long, lest they 'weary and exhaust the patient'; they should use a low and natural tone of voice, and should be serious and earnest but never 'agitated', lest they 'agitate the sick person'.[18]

The Bishop was most concerned that Blacks be informed of their duty to notify the clergy of any cases of sickness, and that the clergy should always inquire of such cases during their visits. He hoped that attorneys and managers would readily co-operate in seeing that due notification was given of sick persons, in accordance with the 67th Canon of the Church of England.[19] In the Bishop's view, then, the visits of the clergy would serve not only as a restraint on the 'profane oath, obscene allusion, scoff of infidel and riot of intemperance',[20] but would also evince their care for the poor and the sick.

For Bishop Coleridge there was a close connection between visiting and preaching in pastoral care. The cottage of the poor and the bedside of the sick and dying were situations for a good preparation for the pulpit. The clergy would be informed of the failures, doubts, weaknesses, trials and afflictions of their parishioners. Also, in the pulpit the clergy should learn to adapt their style of preaching to their congregations; they should be 'colloquial' and 'plain', but never 'vulgar'; their illustrations should be 'local' but not 'personal', for their sermons should be addressed to all people. The Bishop was very much concerned that sermons be scriptural and expository, and that no difficult language should be used. For him, the 'village pulpit' was not a place for controversy but for instruction; it was not a place for attacking the opinions of others in public.[21] He declared, however, that 'the Minister of Christ can never be an indifferent spectator of public opinion'. Rather, it was his duty to guide and even control public opinion by bringing it under the 'mild and holy and wise restraints of religion'. This would involve the minister in much suffering, but he should persevere with a 'sober and clear, and humble, and steady and well-informed mind'.[22]

The Bishop declared that the Gospel had a message of love, holiness and peace for every race, age and condition of men. But 'to the aged African, to the Black born in a state of bondage and still regarded, but by too many, as an inferior being; to the free man whose colour yet marks his African descent, "beautiful" indeed, to adopt the language of the Evangelical Prophet, must be "the feet of him, that bringeth glad tidings of good, that publisheth salvation"'.[23] This is a clear indication of the Bishop's views on the main thrust of sermons, and he was obviously confident that the Blacks would respond to sermons which were pastorally oriented. As he put it on one occasion, 'the Negro especially is peculiarly susceptible of kindness', and would respond to an 'affectionate Minister'.[24]

The Bishop's emphasis on congregational singing must have been motivated by his observation of the Blacks' love of singing which was important for their sense of celebration. He exhorted the clergy to pay more attention to congregational participation in the singing of the Psalms. He regretted that in some places the organ, instead of acting as guide, was a substitute for singing itself. He thought that in other places the Psalms were selected without reference to the service of the day and the chants were unedifying; some unauthorised hymns were also introduced. He impressed upon the clergy that it was their duty to regulate the service, and nothing should be published without their previous knowledge. It was their responsibility to select the Psalms and hymns, as well as the tunes which should be 'plain' and 'congregational'.[25] The Bishop was definite that there should be congregational participation in worship. It was to his credit that a selection of Psalms and hymns with 'appropriate tunes' was made and recommended for use in the Diocese.[26]

Bishop Coleridge constantly faced the challenge of wooing the Blacks away from their practices on Sundays to a strict observance of the Sabbath. The enslaved labourers had Sundays to themselves, and they seized this opportunity to dance and sing, work in their gardens, visit friends on neighbouring estates, trade with them and the poor Whites, and participate in the rites of the obeah cult. The obeah men, the priests of the spirit Obi, who was believed to have come to the West Indies in the minds of the transported Africans, were very powerful. The 'heathen rites' included sacrifices at graves, 'howling and dancing', witchcraft, charms and deadly poisons.[27]

As we have seen in chapter 4, the Rev. William Harte fought hard to instruct enslaved people and encourage a strict observance of the Sabbath in his parish of St. Lucy. The drumming and noise of Sunday dances which began about 4 o'clock disturbed the Church services. Harte tried to stop these dances 'by appealing to a virtually obsolete law of the Island', but he had to give up his efforts because managers told him that they would not co-operate in stopping the dances, and that the enslaved people would have to pay the fines themselves if they were prosecuted.[28] In Harte's lectures is to be found a reference to 'the acknowledged vices of the Negroe character', among which were 'sexual promiscuity, laziness, swearing, stealing and Sabbath-breaking', and 'the vanity of the obeah cult'.[29] Despite Harte's burning desire to evangelise the enslaved population, his views of the African character were similar to those of his White parishioners and the White owners. In the end he had to bow before the power of these White owners and admit that there was no easy remedy for the practices of the enslaved on Sundays.

In 1827 Bishop Coleridge raised the question of the strict observance of the Lord's Day, which should be expected 'under a Christian Government and among Christian people'. He observed that of a population of more than 100,000, not one twenty-fifth were seen in churches on the Sabbath. He regretted that 'God's appointed day of holy rest' was spent in 'worldly business' and in 'hardened indifference'.[30] In 1828 he was pleased to report that a law had recently been passed in Barbados 'for the better observance of the Lord's Day'. He was confident that with the abolition of Sunday markets and the eradication of other practices the character and condition of Blacks would improve, and Christianity would make good progress. He was happy that already there were increased congregations in churches and chapels.[31]

In 1830 the Bishop expressed his disappointment that his earlier expectations had not been realised. He regretted that 'little had been effected towards inducing the Negro to forego his African customs and superstitions'.[32] By 1834, however, he was happy to observe from the Parochial Returns that the Sabbath was better kept and that a large number of adults were under preparation for baptism.[33] The situation had obviously changed during the period of Apprenticeship. But the Bishop was still concerned that a considerable portion of the Black population was unbaptised.[34]

Bishop Coleridge considered the unbaptised 'without the Covenanted pale of salvation'.[35] In his view Baptism 'is the ordinarily appointed instrument whereby we are born again', and as 'the Sacrament of regeneration' it is 'the appointed door of entrance into Christ's Church'.[36] The Bishop expressed his opinion that the right to be baptised should not be confined to the children of 'believers'; the children of 'unbaptized Negroes' who were the property of 'professing Christians' had an equal right to be baptised, according to the rubrics of the Church of England. Both free and enslaved were all sons of 'fallen Adam', and should submit themselves to the same discipline and be born again.[37]

With regard to sponsors (god-parents), the Bishop advised that it would be better to suspend this requirement until adult religious instruction was more advanced, than to allow infants either to die unbaptised or to remain unbaptised for a long period. However, he wished such a suspension of the requirement of sponsors to be exercised only in exceptional circumstances. He thought that the 29th Canon could be relaxed to allow a clergyman to use his discretion in admitting, as sponsors, baptised Blacks who were not yet communicants, but who were at an age of discretion and 'of good report, honest in habit, observers of the Sabbath', and who showed a willingness to profit from the instruction of the minister. Parents were not to act as sponsors of their own children but they had an obligation to be present at the baptism.[38]

On the matter of adult baptism, Bishop Coleridge advised the clergy to be diligent in their preparation of catechumens. In 1830 he expressed his pleasure that there was a marked increase in the number of baptised Blacks as well as in the number of those confirmed.[39] However, he was disappointed that some churches were still without fonts. He insisted that fonts should be provided in all churches, and that they should be built of stone or of some other 'durable material'. They should be of 'sufficient size as to admit of immersion' of the infant, if requested, and should be placed at the western end of churches to symbolise the initiatory nature of the Sacrament.[40] In 1834 the Bishop expressed his satisfaction with the progress made in the matter of adult baptism; he was pleased with this aspect of 'ministerial duty' which had resulted in an increased number of communicants.[41]

Bishop Coleridge's views on the Lord's Supper and the discipline of communicants are worthy of mention. He held that the bread and wine were the 'appointed representations of Christ's death and passion', and 'sure pledges and means whereby the body and blood of Christ are spiritually conveyed to the souls of the faithful'. In this view, he thought that 'the errors of the Romanist and the Socinian' would be avoided.[42] In the matter of discipline, the Bishop advised that if a clergyman had strong reasons for objecting to the character of any person, he would be exercising 'a sound and Christian discretion in fearlessly suspending such individual from the table' until the matter was put before the Spiritual Ordinary (the Bishop). The 'open and notorious evil doer, injurious and revengeful' should be summoned privately and admonished not to present himself at the Lord's Table until he had shown proof of repentance and amendment. The clergy should refer all cases of doubt to the Bishop, and should avoid being 'rigorous' or 'exclusive' in spirit.[43] The Bishop was clearly concerned that the Church's authority should not be used arbitrarily, but that the conscience of the individual should be respected and every effort be made pastorally to lead to his amendment of his way of life.

With regard to the administration of Holy Communion, the Bishop did not advise the clergy to depart from the practice of communicating the Whites first. But he did advise them not to leave a long interval between communicating the Whites and communicating the Blacks.[44] The Bishop, like William Harte (as we have seen in chapter 4), was determined that all classes should approach the Lord's Table on the same occasion, but the practice of administering Holy Communion separately to Whites and to Blacks, however short the interval between, upheld class stratification at the Lord's Supper.

For Bishop Coleridge, marriage was a clear evidence of living the Christian life. In 1829 he regretted to observe from the Parochial Returns that there were rare instances of marriage within the enslaved population, which was a 'neglect of Christian duty' on the part of those baptised. He expressed his awareness of the difficulties concerning marriage. He thought that the promotion of marriage could have been facilitated if 'Managers and other White servants employed by the Planters were generally married persons', if greater care were taken to separate the sexes during working hours, and if the enslaved were encouraged to marry by granting them such incentives as greater domestic comforts, time off to cultivate their own gardens or promotion to positions of trust and authority on estates. The Bishop was disturbed that a Black was allowed to grow up in polygamy and be the father of many children by different women. Yet he considered that an imposition of monogamy upon any Black already practising polygamy might prove too heavy a burden for these reasons: it might lead to a severe struggle between his feelings as a man and his duties as a Christian; it might separate families and render children fatherless; and if the Black was disloyal to his wife then 'we would have converted the ignorant polygamist into the self-convicted adulterer'.[45] However much the Bishop considered polygamy contrary to the spirit of the marriage bond and to the Gospel into which the Blacks had been baptised, he advised a policy of gradualism because of the realities of life among the enslaved population.

The absence of marriage among the enslaved labourers on the Codrington Estates was a constant embarrassment to the SPG. As on other estates in Barbados, polygamy was practised among the Society's enslaved workers. In 1741 Manager Abel Alleyne reported to the Society that polygamy was 'as impossible to prevent as any one thing in the world'; the men were lustful and also hoped to get more food by having more wives.[46] With the appointment of the Rev. John Hothersall Pinder as Chaplain, the SPG had hoped for the promotion of marriages on the Estates. But Pinder was at a loss as to how to act. In 1819 he admitted his inability to encourage marriages of enslaved people and his fear of the prejudices of the White community. He opted for a policy of gradualism, for he considered that Blacks should have time to adopt the discipline of 'Christian culture', and so monogamous marriage should be slowly introduced. Pinder never married anyone. He resigned in 1826 and was succeeded by the Rev. John Packer.

In 1827 Packer married two enslaved Codrington labourers who were given a cottage in the 'new village'. The SPG in 1828 encouraged their Attorney, Forster Clarke, to offer new incentives and asked him and Bishop Coleridge to foster marriages by every means, even if it meant a financial cost to the Society itself. Bishop Coleridge and Forster Clarke offered every married woman free Saturdays throughout the year, and wherever possible they also separated the women from the men at work.[47]

Bishop Coleridge, like Pinder whom he admired, adopted a policy of gradual introduction of monogamous marriage while the Blacks were still in their bondage. He pleaded, 'You must give us time.' However, he was soon able to report to the SPG that he had attended the weddings of 'three respectable couples' who had lived in faithful concubinage for many years, and that two more couples had had their banns read. In 1830 he visited the Codrington Estates and preached on Christian marriage. He informed the SPG that wives would be free before 10 o'clock each morning, in place of their extra free day each fortnight. With an increase in the privileges came an increase in the number of enslaved persons who married each year: twenty-two in 1832, thirty-three in 1833, and about seventy in 1836.[48]

Bishop Coleridge helped to consolidate village and family life on the Codrington Estates during the Apprenticeship period. He moved from a policy of gradualism to one of immediacy as he saw the necessity of monogamous marriage and family life in organising the lives of Blacks in their new status as free men and women. He increased incentives to encourage marriage and even entertained the best 'cottager and his wife' at dinner at Bishop's Court.[49]

The Bishop was still not happy with the situation in the Diocese as a whole. He was anxious to have an increase of marriages, especially among the Black population, but he warned the clergy that they should not be too eager to admit to the 'sacred rite' of Holy Matrimony those 'on whose promise to forsake all former connexions you cannot rely'. He observed that polygamy, 'that almost promiscuous intercourse among the slave population', though considerably checked, still prevailed in almost every part of the Diocese.[50] However, he could take courage from what success he gained among the Blacks on the Codrington Estates and some success elsewhere in Barbados, as a report from one estate indicated.

On this estate there were 412 Blacks, among whom were 61 married couples, and four more couples were expected to be married, 'so your Lordship must see that marriage is now as common on our estates as in any village of England . . . and I must not omit to mention, that many of the couples lately married were young persons who had not lived together before'.[51] This report to the Bishop was obviously intended to demonstrate that the Black was capable of accepting monogamous marriage. But this evidence does not represent an eager and general acceptance of marriage by the Blacks, and there is no doubt that polygamy and faithful concubinage continued to be a challenge to the Church's pastoral care.

Concerning the arrangements for and conduct of the marriage ceremony itself, Bishop Coleridge gave certain directions to the clergy. Very early in his episcopate he insisted that marriages should take place in church and not in private houses, as was the practice among some Whites. He thought that such a practice detracted from the religious nature of the rite, and was in any case contrary to the rubrics of the Church. He maintained that not only should marriages take place in churches and chapels but also between the canonical hours of 8.00 a.m. and 12 noon.[52] In 1830 he was happy to observe from the Parochial Returns that the practice of private marriages had decreased.[53]

The Bishop also gave some clear instructions concerning banns and licences. In publishing the banns of 'Free persons', whether White, Coloured, or Black, the clergy should mention their names and parish or parishes, without distinguishing their colour or condition. In the case of the enslaved people the clergy should designate their parishes as 'this or that Estate' or 'as belonging to this or that Parish', without using the appellation 'slave'.[54] With regard to marriage licences, these were granted by the Governor and were directed to the rector or officiating minister of the parish in which one or both of the parties resided. The custom had, however, arisen for the minister to endorse the licence addressed to him and give it to the parties to be taken to a minister of any other parish in which they might prefer to be married. This provided an opportunity for some 'clandestine' marriages.[55]

Bishop Coleridge was very disturbed by reports that the Civil Ordinary (Governor) had even granted licences to persons under age and to persons within the proscribed degrees of consanguinity. He asserted that a licence dispensed with nothing but the publication of banns, and placed no compulsion on a minister to conduct the marriage. The minister should inquire of the parties, even after they had submitted their licence, whether they knew of any impediment to their union. Such an inquiry was required whether it was a case of banns or licence. In any case, the Bishop was adamant that the practice of endorsing licences should be discontinued, and he reiterated his requirement that a marriage be solemnised within the canonical hours, and in a church or chapel of that parish in which one or both parties resided.[56] The Bishop was clearly concerned that no irregularities be allowed in respect of marriage, which he considered a Christian ideal.

Another matter of concern to the Bishop was the marriage of parties by 'other religious teachers' who had no legal authority. He informed his clergy that in cases of separation between such parties, which were 'not uncommon', they would be called upon 'to unite in a fresh and legal marriage' an individual who had formerly been 'joined' to another by the Moravian or Wesleyan missionary. He advised them to make a careful inquiry concerning the grounds of separation, as well as concerning the civil conditions (whether free or bond) of the persons involved. If they could obtain no guidance from the Colonial Act concerning re-marriage, then they should follow the Common Law of the land, and any objectors would have to indicate the 'local' law that was being infringed.[57] In this whole matter we see that only the Established Clergy at that time had legal status in the performance of certain pastoral duties'. We also see the consistent attitude of Bishop Coleridge towards the ministry of other denominations.

From marriages we come finally to a consideration of funerals. As we noticed earlier, the Bishop considered the practices of Blacks in respect of the dead to be superstitious. He could not understand their 'howling and dancing', and their sacrifices at the graves of the dead. In 1830 he was pleased to observe that the practice of obeah was dying away, 'and the superstitious fear of its effects is decreasing with the increase of knowledge and religion'. To him it was a relief that 'nightly howling over the dead and wakes' were rarely heard, and that 'the custom, brought from Africa, of offering meats at the graves of the deceased' had ceased or was practised only 'by stealth'.[58] The Bishop also expressed his pleasure that the enslaved people were being given 'proper' burials.[59] Whether or not some funeral customs continued to be practised stealthily, it is certain that wakes survived well into our own times.

Concerning the times and places of funerals, the Bishop gave some instructions to the clergy. He advised that funerals should take place in daylight and the service should be properly conducted. A controversy arose when the 'corpse of a respectable Lady was refused participation in those holy Ceremonies', much to the distress of her relatives and friends. There was a plea for a modification of the Bishop's ruling, to allow the doors of parish churches to be opened at all times for funerals. The Bishop reiterated his decision that a corpse should not be brought into church after the time he had stipulated. He also stated that this regulation could only be relaxed in times of epidemic disease or in some extraordinary circumstances.[60] In 1830 he was happy to note the improvement in the punctuality and conduct of funerals. He, however, regretted that the practice of burial in private places still existed.

The custom of family burial grounds had been adopted by the early settlers of the island and the Bishop thought that it should be discontinued. He was equally adamant in his opinion that burials in churches and chapels should cease, for this bred superstition and constituted a danger to the health of the living in times of 'contagious distempers'.[61] The Bishop certainly was not prepared to grant any concessions with regard to the funerals and burials of the privileged.

Bishop Coleridge was consistent in his policy that the Church's pastoral care should be for all classes. In his view, the clergyman was a 'Pastor of all' and should be found in 'cottage and mansion, neither despising the poverty of the one, nor seduced, from the strictness of his calling, by the blandishments of the other'. The clergyman should see the schools as 'spiritual nurseries: the seed-plots of that future harvest of matured holiness'. In baptising, marrying, churching of women (giving thanks to God for childbirth), burying, presiding at the Vestry and mediating between contending parties, he should prove himself a reconciling and faithful steward of God.[62]

Bishop Coleridge recognised the African customs as being a particular challenge to the Church's pastoral care. In emphasising particularly the importance of religious instruction, the strict observance of the Sabbath, the necessity of baptism, the ideal of monogamous marriage and the proper conduct of funerals, he hoped to civilise and evangelise the enslaved Africans.

# 7

# SOCIAL REFORM
## GRADUAL AND PEACEFUL

AS WE HAVE SEEN, the major thrust of Bishop Coleridge's episcopate was the amelioration and evangelisation of the enslaved population. He received the full support of the British government, religious societies, the local legislature, and local organisations devoted to the religious instruction and amelioration of the lot of the labouring class. He also won the confidence and co-operation of various proprietors, and was fully involved in promoting the great social reform leading to Emancipation and Apprenticeship, particularly on the Codrington Estates which in large measure served as a model for other estates on the island.

The SPG looked to Bishop Coleridge for leadership in implementing certain measures that would lead to the gradual emancipation of their enslaved labourers on the Codrington Estates. In 1831 they gave instructions that the whipping of enslaved women should be abolished and that all punishment should be administered according to a procedure which was formalised and could be openly witnessed. They also gave orders to teach writing and arithmetic in the schools; to grant manumissions, whenever possible, to enslaved workers of good report; to permit enslaved people to purchase their freedom from enforced labour for one or more days of the week; to manumit enslaved persons who purchased their freedom for six working days of the week; to permit children born in wedlock to inherit the free days earned by their parents, provided that the Society was given proportionate relief from the support of the children; to make it known that enslaved people were attached to the soil and could not be sold; to introduce task labour on the Estates, to give each enslaved person specific tasks, and to begin substituting hired labour for enslaved labour by paying the enslaved people for their work on 'free' days.'[1]

Bishop Coleridge informed the Society that these measures were received in the West Indies with mixed sentiments. Some predicted the ruin of the Estates and the College, while others welcomed the regulations and looked forward to the benefits they would produce. Some felt that the Society had a control of their enslaved workers which other proprietors did not have; others again declared that they were embarrassed by debt and could only make some experiments.

Bishop Coleridge summoned about eleven of the most influential enslaved persons on the Codrington Estates and their driver, Jack Robin, to meet with himself, the attorney, Forster Clarke, Manager Hinkson and the new chaplain, the Rev. Thomas Watts. The Bishop read the new regulations introduced by the Society and asked for comments from the enslaved workers. As he reported, the enslaved showed 'no want to shrewdness'. It was clear that they understood the significance of each regulation. They were encouraged that the Bishop and the Society would regularly inspect the register of punishments, but were unimpressed with the regulation that they should never be sold for, as the Bishop observed, they '. . . felt themselves all along for a long time as virtually attached to the soil'.[2] The Bishop's own understanding of the new regulations was that they would teach the enslaved people habits of thrift and self-reliance, get them accustomed to working for wages and commit them to remaining attached to the Estates after they were emancipated.[3]

This new plan for gradual manumission met with very partial success. Only four enslaved persons were manumitted before the event of general emancipation. Two purchased their freedom outside of the terms of the new plan, while two others availed themselves of the new regulations. The high expectations which were held for the big success of the new measures were frustrated partly by the devastations caused on the Estates by the terrible hurricane of 11 August 1831.[4]

In 1832 the Society resolved to implement another plan for the gradual emancipation of their enslaved workers. They introduced the allotment system whereby a cottage and plot of land would be given to each Black family to provide for the subsistence of its members. In return, their labour on the Estates would be regarded as payment of rent. This new measure gave the Blacks the status of virtual serfs. Nine families were selected to start the experiment, and in 1833 Bishop Coleridge was happy to report that they were zealously planting their allotments and building their houses, and were working on the Estates as enthusiastically as they did on their own plots.

In 1834 Chaplain Watts reported that the cottagers no longer drew their supplies from the Estates; they had a good crop of corn and potatoes. Watts also reported that they had completed four houses which looked 'remarkably neat and comfortable'. Bishop Coleridge and Watts began to select couples whom they considered industrious and worthy of grants when emancipation came. The attorney, Forster Clarke, expressed his satisfaction with the allotment system which he thought was the only plan by which the Blacks in Barbados could be civilised and settled happily.[5]

The success of the allotment system on the Codrington Estates did prepare the way for the orderly acceptance of emancipation by the Society's enslaved labourers. Through the undaunted efforts of emancipationists in England, like William Wilberforce, and the reforming zeal of Lord Stanley, Secretary of State for the Colonies, emancipation was achieved. Stanley's bill was passed as the Emancipation Act on the 28th of August 1833, a month after Wilberforce's death, and the Act became effective on 1 August 1834. The Act provided that (i) a sum of £20,000,000 be granted to the West Indian planters by the British government as compensation for losses incurred by the emancipation of their enslaved labourers; (ii) enslavement be abolished with effect from 1 August 1834, and children under the age of six years be granted their immediate freedom; (iii) enslaved people generally be not given their full freedom immediately, but a period of apprenticeship be introduced – six years for field labourers and four years for domestic servants; (iv) the working week for apprentices be reduced to forty-five hours and Sunday labour be abolished; (v) wages be paid for labour exceeding 45 hours a week, and apprentices be able to purchase their freedom before the period of apprenticeship was terminated, at which time full freedom would be obtained; (vi) special magistrates be appointed, their salaries being paid by the British government, to ensure that the provisions of the Act, with regard to the apprentices, were strictly observed;

(vii) allowances, previously granted to enslaved workers, be continued during the period of apprenticeship.[6]

On the whole, the Apprenticeship system was intended to make the transition from enslavement to freedom a smooth and peaceful one, to ensure that there would be sufficient labour on the plantations for some years to come, and to prepare the apprentices for their responsibilities as free citizens.[7] It has been observed that Bishop Coleridge's leadership of the Anglican Church in Barbados and in other territories of his Diocese contributed a great deal to the peaceful inauguration of this new epoch for the enslaved population.[8]

Barbados' share of the grant to compensate West Indian planters was £1,721,345.19s.7d. sterling.[9] The SPG received £8,823.8s.9d. for its 411 enslaved workers. The programme of breeding enslaved workers after the abolition of the slave trade in 1807 had borne great results in Barbados, and on the Codrington Estates in particular. To Coleridge the compensation which the SPG received seemed indeed handsome.[10]

There was not much material change in the order of things on the Codrington Estates during the period of apprenticeship, 1834–38. The Blacks were entitled by law to their usual provisions from the Estates. In 1837 and 1838 the SPG's expenditure for the maintenance of 318 labourers and their 125 children was approximately £1,875 per annum. This sum included the cost of food provisions, medical care, clothing, housing materials and gratuities. In return for their support, the apprenticed Blacks had to work on the Estates as formerly. It was in the hours of work that a substantial change was made. If the apprentices worked for more than forty-five hours a week they received wages from the Estates. For instance, during 1837 the apprentices earned £293.3s.6d. for overtime work.[11]

The allotment system proved the most significant innovation on the Codrington Estates during the Apprenticeship period. The Society wished this system to be the model for the future. By 1836 twenty families (80 persons) had been settled as cottagers, and the manager, Thomas King, expressed the hope that the whole population would be settled on land they could consider their own. The cottagers co-operated fully. Their behaviour was reportably better than that of the other Blacks, and their dress showed that they took some pride in their personal appearance. Their sense of pride was also demonstrated by the tidiness of their houses. On the whole, they seemed happy to provide for themselves, while working for the estates. They cultivated ginger, sugar cane and arrowroot to raise some cash, while growing their own food provisions, and kept sheep, pigs and poultry.[12] The allotment system was successfully establishing a Black tenantry in relation to the Codrington Estates.

Elsewhere in Barbados there was much strife, as the planters complained that the system of apprenticeship was too costly, the apprentices could not give their labour to employers of their choice, and the Special Magistrates pleased neither planters nor apprentices. While there were bad relationships between planters and apprentices in Barbados, this system was working well on the Codrington Estates, and the system of allotment was likely to attract the attention of all planters over the island. The Blacks themselves were obviously happy with the allotment system, and it promised to provide a stable supply of labour and lessen cash expenditures by substituting land in part for cash as a means of compensating the Blacks.

Both Bishop Coleridge and the SPG commended the allotment system which they thought would keep the social order intact, help to sustain and strengthen the Black communities and families, and inculcate in them the virtues of independent landholders, while keeping them dependent on proprietors. As has been stated, Bishop Coleridge and the SPG 'hoped to transplant to Barbados and the West Indies the paternalistic social structure of an ideal English village'.[13]

The Apprenticeship system was not generally successful in Barbados. In fact, there was some open opposition to it. Robert Bowcher Clarke, the Solicitor General, argued in the House of Assembly that the system brought no honour to the Barbadian planter and should therefore be abolished. Clarke contended that the apprentices should be completely emancipated on 1 August 1838. Some opposing resolutions were tabled, but Clarke won the day. His loyal supporter, James Sarsfield Bascom, gave notice that a Bill should be introduced to terminate the apprenticeship of praedial labourers on the proposed date, and that a committee should be appointed by the Council to meet with them to prepare the Bill. Clarke fell ill but Bascom continued to pilot the Bill, which was introduced on 15 May 1838. It successfully passed all stages in the House, and was sent to the Council where it received the same favourable acceptance. On the following day, 16 May, the Governor gave his assent. This important Act (1 Victoria, Cap. 32 of the Colonial Acts) declared that all praedial, apprenticed labourers in the island should be freed from 1 August 1838; that any former praedial labourers who were willing to continue their former work for agreed wages should not be ejected or expelled from their plantations before 1 November; that proprietors should provide for such apprentices as were rendered incapacitated by disease, or were otherwise incapable of earning their living, or until adequate provisions could be made for them by law. If such apprentices, however, had relations, they should be maintained by them from 1 August 1839. Following upon the successful termination of Apprenticeship, Robert Bowcher Clarke remonstrated against the four per cent duty which had been imposed on the items which the planters exported. This duty was abolished by an Act of the Imperial Parliament on 14 August 1838, and its place was taken by a duty on essential goods consumed by both planters and labourers.[14]

The Colonial legislature acted, without compulsion from the British Parliament, in providing for the termination of Apprenticeship. Planters became eager to anticipate the new local law. One planter even emancipated his labourers before the effective date for the termination of apprenticeship. On 29 May 1838, Bishop Coleridge therefore informed the SPG that he had decided to liberate their apprentices on the following day. Both the Bishop and the SPG had been anxious to grant these apprentices unrestricted freedom as soon as possible, and as peacefully as possible.'

On Wednesday, 30 May, the Bishop visited the attorney, Thomas G. King, Esq., at his residence at 12 noon. The labourers assembled before the attorney's residence, and the Bishop explained to them the purpose of the meeting, and assured them that they would be freed in such a manner as not to cause any distress to the aged and infirm. The people responded enthusiastically, and the Bishop was considered 'clear, kind and impressive'. He reminded them that it was now thirteen years since his arrival in Barbados, and that his primary object had been 'to benefit both their souls and bodies'. Indeed, he informed them that it was his intention from the first to promote the general welfare of the Barbadian community by demonstrating their amelioration as a model. He confessed that he had to wait for opportunities, so as not to cause jealousy in the island and thus defeat his purpose. He referred to the benefits granted to the married women, the allotment or 'cottier', system and other measures of 'partial freedom', which had proved models for adoption on other estates on the island. He said that if anyone challenged him as to why he did not press for emancipation sooner, he would maintain that he 'had watched the time'. Also, he would defend his anticipation of the official date of emancipation by stating that in some quarters an alternative date was being mentioned, and 'he did not wish to keep them in an unsettled state'.[17]

Bishop Coleridge further informed the assembled labourers that he did not wish 'the Society's people to be behind others, but rather in the van of improvement'. He proceeded to read the Proclamations recently issued by the Governor in Council concerning the termination of Apprenticeship. He also read a written Agreement which, with the attorney, Mr. King, he was about to sign, to obtain their freedom and privileges, as if conferred by an Act of the island. After explaining the Agreement, the Bishop mentioned the rates of wages which, as free labourers, they would receive in cash, or in houses and extra allotments of land in the case of cottagers. These wages would vary according to the nature and efficiency of the work done. Those who continued to work for the Estates would keep their houses and land and would receive medical care, free of cost. The Bishop concluded by expressing his confidence in them, and his hope that he would be able to state proudly at the meeting of Council on the following Tuesday that 'they behaved well under this great change'. The people expressed their gratitude to him and assured him of their good behaviour. The Bishop and Mr. King then signed the Agreement before them, in the presence of Captain Coppage, the Special Magistrate of the district, and many other witnesses, among whom were the Archdeacon of Barbados, the Rector of St. John, the Principal and Tutor of the College and the Chaplain of the Estates.[18]

After the signing of the Agreement, the Bishop informed the people of the provisions which would be allowed for the week and of presents which would be given them at Whitsuntide, in addition to their wages. He also informed them that the new system of free labour would begin by the 4th June following. He then dismissed them with a 'solemn exhortation' to remember that 'every good gift was from above', and that they should therefore meet in the 'House of God' on the following Sunday, when he hoped to be present, to thank God for their gift of freedom. They were given the rest of the day off, and they spent it 'in orderly and cheerful amusement in the mill-yard, going home at an early hour'. The number of those freed was 288. Seven infirm and thirteen aged persons were to continue for life in the care of the Society, with the one condition that the aged performed such work on the Estates as they were able.[19]

The plan for managing the Codrington Estates on the basis of free labour was drawn up by the agricultural attorney, Thomas King. The field labourers were to receive wages ranging from 5s. a week for inferior labourers to 6s.3d. a week for the 'effective' ones. Each couple would have a house and a third of an acre of land. Their children would be paid 7½d. a day. Bishop Coleridge supported this system of 'located labour', and was happy that it proved a model for adoption very generally in the island. In fact, the system was firmly established by the Masters and Servants Act of 1840, and it continued in substance until it was abolished in 1937.[20] Both in the allotment system during the period of apprenticeship and in the located labour system after emancipation the Codrington Estates under the leadership of the Bishop and the agricultural attorneys provided models of social change, though they were almost feudal in character.

In order to establish themselves as free citizens in society and in a free economy, it was important that the Blacks acquire the discipline of thrift. As part of their plan to free their enslaved workers gradually, the SPG had established a savings bank at Codrington in 1831 to encourage them to save something from their small incomes. Seventeen of them deposited a total of £2.10s. sterling, while others promised to make deposits from the sale of their goods. However, the extensive damage caused by the hurricane of that same year forced the first customers to withdraw their savings, and the Blacks showed no renewed interest in saving through the bank. They preferred to make money by the sale of their poultry and livestock.[21]

Bishop Coleridge was very concerned that the Blacks should learn to be thrifty, and so he promoted the formation of Friendly Societies. By 1834 four Societies were established with about 1,599 members.[22] During the apprenticeship period membership of Friendly Societies increased greatly and in 1837 the Bishop was happy to observe from the Parochial Returns that total membership stood at 4,590, and that people were paying their contributions even when their goods were scarce. The Bishop was satisfied that the Blacks were becoming 'industrious', and he was hopeful that 'such institutions may become powerful auxiliaries to the advancement of Christian knowledge'.[23]

With regard to medical care, a Medical Dispensary Society was formed during Bishop Coleridge's episcopate. On 4 June 1840, an Act 'for incorporating the members of a Society for the establishment and maintenance of an hospital for the reception and treatment of the sick poor' passed the legislature. Subsequently, buildings were erected at a cost of about £3,850 sterling, which was raised by voluntary subscriptions in Barbados and in England. On 1 July 1844, the General Hospital was opened. Coleridge's successor as Bishop of the Diocese (his former Archdeacon, Thomas Parry) served as one of the Trustees of the new hospital, and the clergy of St. Michael's in turn performed the duties of Chaplain.[24] Closely related to medical care was the provision of an Asylum for the Coloured poor.

Bishop Coleridge was also involved in providing care and better conditions for prisoners. In 1835 it was stipulated that the administration of the Common Gaol should be vested in a Board of Superintendence, comprising the Bishop of the Diocese, or in his absence the Archdeacon, or in the latter's absence the Rural Dean of the island; the Honourable President of the Council, the Speaker of the House of Assembly, the three police magistrates of Bridgetown for the time being, two members of Council, and two members of the House of Assembly to be nominated by the Governor or Commander-in-Chief of the Island, for the time being. The terms of reference of the Board were the improvement of the Gaol buildings and facilities for the prisoners. In particular, the Board was to request the Town Hall Committee to take action and the Provost Marshal to appoint a gaoler. A clergyman of the Church of England was to be appointed as Chaplain to the Gaol to read prayers to the prisoners at least twice during the week and on Sundays, Christmas Day, and Good Friday; the Chaplain would also visit, with free access to the prisoners. If any prisoner was a 'Dissenter' or a 'Catholic', the Provost Marshal was to give him permission to communicate with his respective minister. The Governor or Commander-in-Chief was to appoint the Chaplain, who would receive a salary of £50 per annum from the Treasury. A doctor was also to be appointed and to receive a salary from the Treasury. The Rev. William Harte and John Cutting, Esq., MD, were the first Chaplain and medical attendant respectively to be appointed by the Governor under an Act of Legislature entitled, 'An Act for the better Regulating the common Gaol in this Island'. Other stipulations in the reform of the Gaol were the separation of men from women, the prohibition of gambling, and the provision of 'plain and wholesome' food, fresh air and exercise.[25]

By the time the Blacks were granted full freedom, there were certain social institutions established, or in the process of being established, to enable them to organise their lives in a free society in which the practice of thrift would be important, and in which care in hospital, asylum and prison might be required. In all these, as well as in the provision of those institutions related to the education of the Blacks,[26] Bishop Coleridge was active. He could be pleased that his consistent policy of amelioration and evangelisation had contributed to the gradual and peaceful emancipation of Blacks in Barbados and elsewhere in his Diocese. His own description of that epoch-making occasion of the emancipation of the enslaved people in the West Indies is worthy of quotation:

> In one day – in one moment – was this great measure carried into execution. Eight hundred thousand human beings lay down at night as slaves, and rose in the morning as free as ourselves. It might have been expected that on such an occasion there would have been some outburst of public feeling. I was present but there was no gathering that affected the public peace. There was a gathering: but it was a gathering of young and old together, in the house of the common Father of all. It was my peculiar happiness on that ever memorable day, to address a congregation of nearly 4,000 persons, of whom more than 3,000 were negroes just emancipated. And such was the order, such the deep attention and perfect silence, that . . . you might have heard a pin drop. Among this mass of people, of all colours, were thousands of my African brethren, joining with their European brother, in offering up their prayers and thanksgivings to the Father, Redeemer and Sanctifier of all. To prepare the minds of a mass of persons, so peculiarly situated, for a change such as this, was a work requiring the exercise of great patience and altogether of a most arduous nature. And it was chiefly owing to the Society for the Propagation of the Gospel that that day not only passed in peace, but was distinguished for the proper feeling that prevailed and its perfect order.[27]

# 8

## RETURN TO ENGLAND
## MISSION ACCOMPLISHED

BECAUSE OF FAILING HEALTH, in 1841 Bishop Coleridge was compelled to leave Barbados and his Diocese and return to England. On 11 June in that year one of his relatives, F.G. Coleridge, wrote from Ottery St. Mary to the Rev. John Keble, informing him that the Bishop was expected home at the end of July, and that the Bishop was building a house at Salston.[1] From this house the Bishop himself wrote to John Keble in 1846 to thank him for a copy of his *Lyra Innocentium*.[2]

On the Bishop's departure from the Diocese it was administered by the three archdeacons with whom he had already shared many of his administrative duties. For the Archdeaconry of Barbados (including the Windward Islands) there was the Venerable Thomas Parry; for the Archdeaconry of Antigua (including the Leeward Islands), the Venerable Daniel Gateward Davis; and for the Archdeaconry of British Guiana, the Venerable William Piercy Austin.

On Bishop Coleridge's formal resignation in 1842, the Diocese was divided into three Sees corresponding to the archdeaconries mentioned above, and the three archdeacons were appointed respectively to these Sees. They were consecrated, together with the Bishops of Gibraltar and Tasmania, in Westminster Abbey on 21 August 1842. Bishop Coleridge preached the sermon at this Consecration, in which he stressed the need for Britain to provide for the spiritual welfare of its growing Empire, and the importance of episcopal direction in the Church in the Colonies.[3] Other sentiments expressed in his sermon were similar to those which he had stressed in the previous year in his sermon at the Consecration of George Augustus Selwyn as Bishop of New Zealand.

Among other statements, he had mentioned the 'ignorance, superstitious fears; immoral usages and unbridled passions' of 'the savage man in his native wilds'.[4] This is a clear reference to the African customs and practices against which he had struggled in his own episcopate and against which he thought his episcopal brethren should continue to fight.

Thomas Parry was Bishop of Barbados from 1842 to 1870; Daniel Gateward Davis was Bishop of Antigua from 1842 to 1857, and William Piercy Austin was Bishop of British Guiana from 1842 to 1892. It was to Bishop Coleridge's credit that he had selected three able men as archdeacons, who could immediately succeed him as bishops of new Sees created out of the same archdeaconries.

In his retirement Bishop Coleridge was involved, with his cousin Edward Coleridge, in plans for the establishment of a missionary college. In 1843 Edward Coleridge, Assistant-Master and Fellow of Eton, wrote to John Keble concerning the need for an adequate supply of ministers, 'duly prepared in heart and mind', to labour in the 'dependencies of the British Empire'. He proposed that an appropriate education should be provided, which would embrace all the benefits offered by the ancient universities of England to candidates for Holy Orders, but 'at less expense and with greater simplicity and frugality of habits'. He also stated that candidates should be drawn from the 'pupils of our endowed Grammar Schools' whose masters had expressed the hope that some missionary students would go forth from their walls.

Edward Coleridge went on to propose that a college be founded at Oxford or Cambridge, or in some other suitable place, to educate and train such young men as might be willing to dedicate themselves to the ministry of the Church in the British Colonies. He was confident that such an institution would meet with the approval of colonial bishops, especially when they learned that the project had sprung in large measure from the suggestions of the Bishops of Australia, New Zealand, and Tasmania respectively. He thought that the colonial bishops would also give their assent when they heard that the institution would be under the 'immediate management and control' of Bishop Coleridge who had expressed his willingness to assume the office of 'Honorary Principal'.[5]

After stating the estimated size of the institution (Chapel, Hall, apartments for 50 students at first but ultimately for 200, quarters for officers and servants), Edward Coleridge mentioned that the required money should be raised from donations and subscriptions. With regard to the curriculum, he thought that it should be like that of an English university, with the addition of those aspects of training that would prepare students for the mission-field. For instance, students should be taught the importance of congregational singing; they should acquire a 'moderate but sound knowledge of medicine' and the more common operations of surgery such as 'Bleeding and Vaccination'; they should be frugal in their habits; they should be regular in their attendance at the daily services of the Church; they should go to bed early and rise early in the morning. As Edward Coleridge saw it, such discipline should be taught as would 'bring up the Inmates in a proper degree of hardness, and to fit them for their future labours, and for the peculiar duties they will have to discharge'.[6] One cannot fail to sense that these views of Edward Coleridge reflected the experience of Bishop Coleridge, and that the proposed curriculum for a missionary college drew heavily from that of Codrington College.

Edward Coleridge received warm support for his project which also met with the approval of the Archbishops of Canterbury and York and the Bishop of London. A missionary college was eventually founded at St. Augustine's, Canterbury, in 1848, with Bishop Coleridge as the first Warden.[7] He must have been happy to contribute towards the training of clergy for service in the British Colonies – a cause which was dear to his heart. His involvement in the life and work of Codrington College would also have stood him in good stead as the pioneering Warden of St. Augustine's College. He served in this capacity until his death on 21 December 1849.

From the time he answered the call to serve as the first Bishop in the newly created See of Barbados and the Leeward Islands until he died, William Hart Coleridge was zealous for the ministry of the Church of England in the British dependencies. To his lot had fallen a number of West Indian colonies which comprised his large Diocese. In this study we have concentrated on his episcopate in the island of Barbados, but the effects of his leadership can be seen in the administration and development of those other parts of the Diocese which became separate Sees when he resigned.

Bishop Coleridge adhered firmly to the main purpose of his appointment as a Colonial Bishop – the amelioration of the Black population. Like Christopher Lipscomb, his fellow-Bishop of the See of Jamaica, he was conveyed with full honours to his Diocese where he and his party received an enthusiastic reception from high and low alike. There was the sense that a new era had dawned on the island.

As far as the Governor was concerned there was indeed a new situation, for he had hitherto held the full powers of Ordinary. As we have seen, the new Bishop pressed for a definition of his jurisdiction as a Colonial Bishop, particularly in the matter of nominating and collating clergymen to vacant benefices. The British Government laid down some guidelines which included the right of the Bishop to nominate to the Governor a clergyman who had been resident in his Diocese for at least six months before the vacancy occurred. From the Letters Patent the Bishop had power to collate, but collation was divided into two parts, 'Presentation and Institution', thus establishing the Bishop's full jurisdiction, while not embarrassing the Governor.

By making a tour of his Diocese, Bishop Coleridge obtained first-hand knowledge of its condition. In Barbados he found eleven parish churches, but he considered these inadequate for the Church's outreach among the labouring class. He set about a massive programme of providing more places of worship both in the urban and rural areas. The plans which had been conceived before his arrival in the island for another Church in Bridgetown were brought to birth by him, and St. Mary's Chapel was built. The results of his building programme were, however, seen in the erection of Chapels of Ease with their Romantic Gothic Revival style, which was adopted for the building of chapels by all denominations for over a century.

In his building programme, Bishop Coleridge was undaunted by the terrible hurricane of 11 August 1831 which devastated the island. With generous support from the SPG, the SPCK, and other subscriptions from Britain, as well as grants from the local Legislature and other local subscriptions, he was able to rebuild those Chapels of Ease which had been destroyed. With a favourable response to his request that seven of the parish churches be rebuilt from the balance of the Parliamentary Relief Grant, he was able to restore these places of worship also. He continued to provide more Chapels of Ease serving defined districts with their own curates, but very much subject to the superintendence of the rectors of the parish churches. Another of Bishop Coleridge's innovations was the creation of Chapel-Schools which served the dual purpose of worship on Sundays and education during the week. The majority of these Chapel-Schools were later consecrated as full chapels.

It was by the establishment of new places of worship that Bishop Coleridge sought to provide increased accommodation – particularly for the labouring class – and in this he was successful. Distinctions were none the less maintained in the seating of Whites, Coloureds and Blacks in Church. Pews were reserved for pew-renters, and this system was not discontinued by the Bishop. The Free Coloureds and the Blacks were relegated to the back of the Church and to the gallery. If pews were not occupied by their renters, then it was not surprising that Free Coloureds and Blacks sought to use them, causing much tension between themselves and the Whites from time to time.

Bishop Coleridge saw early that the great task of amelioration and evangelisation required the delegation of authority, and the recruitment and training of an adequate number of clergy. The British Government provided him with two archdeacons, one for Barbados and one for Antigua. That section of his Diocese in British Guiana which was at first administered by his Commissary, was eventually raised to an archdeaconry. The Bishop further delegated authority by introducing the office of Rural Dean, as was the practice in England.

Closely related to his delegation of administrative responsibilities was the Bishop's policy of recruiting clergy. He found fifteen clergy in Barbados on his arrival. Initially he recruited more candidates for the ministry from the universities of Oxford and Cambridge and from Trinity College, Dublin. But he became convinced that the stability and continuity of the ministry would depend on candidates recruited locally and trained locally. This conviction led him to re-organise Codrington College on the lines of the original intention of the Testator, Christopher Codrington. The SPG had every confidence in Bishop Coleridge and were themselves taking steps to have the College re-organised. It was a triumph for both the SPG and

Bishop Coleridge when Codrington College was opened as a theological college in 1830 to serve the region. From the College went forth many Barbadians to serve in the far-flung Diocese. At the end of his episcopate the clergy in Barbados had increased from fifteen to twenty-nine. The College provided not only theological education but also education in Classics, Mathematics, Logic and some subjects in Science and Medicine. It grew to the status of a University College, and today it maintains an affiliation with the University of Durham and with the University of the West Indies.

Bishop Coleridge considered public education integral to amelioration and evangelisation. The consolidation of Parochial Schools, and the provision of National Schools, Infant, Estate, and Sunday Schools were all directed to this end. With the development of Central Schools and the Harrison Free School, which later became Secondary Schools (Combermere, Queen's College and Harrison College), and the re-organisation of Codrington College, Bishop Coleridge laid the foundations for primary, secondary and tertiary education in Barbados.

Hand in hand with the civilising influence of education was the Church's pastoral care which, Bishop Coleridge insisted, should be for all classes. He was particularly concerned to meet the challenge of such African customs as the desecration of the Sabbath, the cult of obeah, superstition, polygamy and concubinage. In his guidance to his clergy in the many aspects of pastoral care he showed his concern about these practices. With the religious instruction of the Blacks, particularly by the readers and catechists who were 'auxiliaries' to the clergy, and with the increase in the number of those baptised, there was some improvement in the observance of the Sabbath. But polygamy and concubinage persisted. Bishop Coleridge felt that monogamous marriage should be introduced gradually, while the Blacks were still in their state of bondage. During the period of Apprenticeship, however, he was more urgent in his promotion of monogamous marriage, and on the Codrington Estates he established many incentives to marriage and granted benefits to married couples. His policy met with some success at Codrington, but there was no enthusiastic and general acceptance of monogamous marriage among the Black population. Indeed, faithful concubinage has continued into this century. So too have the cult of obeah, wakes for the dead, and other African customs which have survived from one generation to another through secret meetings, ceremonies and rituals.[8]

It was on the Codrington Estates that the Bishop's involvement in the great social reform of Emancipation and Apprenticeship could directly be seen. It was to his leadership and that of their agricultural attorneys that the SPG looked for the implementation of measures for the gradual emancipation of those enslaved on their plantations. The systems of allotment and located labour proved successful, despite their semi-feudal character, and were adopted in other estates in the island.

Bishop Coleridge had adopted a policy of gradualism in this matter of emancipation, but his leadership right up to the abolition of slavery on 1 August 1834, and during the period of preparation for total emancipation, was dynamic and effective. It was a tribute to his leadership that those enslaved at Codrington were freed peacefully on 30 May 1838, before the legal date of Emancipation. It was a tribute to his leadership in the Anglican Church generally that the Blacks in Barbados and elsewhere in his Diocese celebrated the Day of Emancipation, 1 August 1838, joyfully and peacefully, and that they had certain social institutions to help them settle as free citizens. Despite his failing health, Bishop Coleridge must have returned to England with a sense of a mission accomplished.

# APPENDIX 1

## Building Funds: Source and Use

### From Statement of Returns, 1837 (USPG Archives)

*Important financial note*:

£1/–/– sterling = £ 1/10/– currency. Figures below are in '£ currency' as this was clearly the basis of calculation, e.g. grant to St. Mary's (below) of £3,333/6/8 sterling was actually £5,000 currency.

| Number of Buildings | Capacity of Buildings | Use | Source | Amount |
|---|---|---|---|---|
| 25 | 6,512 | BUILDING AND REPAIRING SCHOOLS £15,860 | FROM THE MOTHER COUNTRY £38,141 | HURRICANE SUBSCRIPTION FUND £14,628 |
| 5 | 1,025 | CHAPEL-SCHOOL £1,870 | | PARLIAMENTARY HURRICANE FUND £7,350 |
| 10 | 9,391 | | | WEST INDIAN BUILDING FUND £4,528 |
| | | | | S.P.G. £6,065* *Including £2,000 for 'their Chapel'. |
| 11 | 10,640 | BUILDING AND REPAIRING CHAPELS £28,409 | FROM THE COLONY £44,882 | PARLIAMENTARY GRANT TO ST MARY'S £5,000 |
| | | | | COLONIAL LEGISLATURE GRANT TO ST MARY'S £5,000 |
| | | REBUILDING AND REPAIRING PARISH CHURCHES £36,904 | | PAROCHIAL TAXATION AND PRIVATE SUBSCRIPTIONS £36,382 |
| 51 | 27,578 | £83,023 | | £83,023 |

# Appendix II

## Clergy (Status in Italic)

| | MOTHER COUNTRY | COLONY | CODR'TON TRUST EXTATES |
|---|:---:|:---:|:---:|
| Bishop        W.H. Coleridge, D.D. | X | | |
| Archdeacon    E. Elliot, B.D. | X | | |
| Rural Dean    J.H. Gittens, B.A. *(see below)* | | | |
| **ST. MICHAEL** | | | |
|   W. Garnett *R* | | X | |
|   W.M. Harte *A/C* | X | | |
|   G.P. Culpeper *A/C* | X | | |
|   C.C.Cummins *A/C* | X | | |
|   J.H. Nurse, B.A. *A/C* | X | | |
|   T.Rowe *A/C & Master at Harrison's Free School* | | X | |
|   W. Gill *A/C* | | X | |
|   J.F.Barrow, B.A. *A/C* | | X | |
|   W.H. Bovell, B.A. *Bishop's Chaplain* | X | | |
|   T. Gill, M.A. *Garrison Chaplain* | X | | |
| **CHRIST CHURCH** | | | |
|   C.C. Gill *R* | | X | |
|   J.Gittens *A/C* | X | | |
| **ST. PHILIP** | | | |
|   R.F. King *R* | | X | |
|   T. Clarke, B/A/ *A/C* | X | | |
| **ST. JOHN** | | | |
|   J.H. Gittens *R & R.D.* | | X | |
|   S.A. Farr *A/C & Master at Codrington School* | | X | |
|   H. Jones, M.A. *Principal of Codrington School* | | | X |
|   E.P. Smith, M.A. *Tutor at Codrington College* | | | X |
|   T. Watts *Master at Codrington School* | | | X |
| **ST. GEORGE** | | | |
|   W. Pinder, M.A. *R* | | X | |
|   J.K. Went, B.A. *A/C* | X | | |
|   E. Lovell *A/C* | X | | |
| **ST. THOMAS** | | | |
|   J. Packer *R* | | X | |
| **ST. JAMES** | | | |
|   G.F. Maynard *R* | | X | |
| **ST. PETER** | | | |
|   W.D. Sealy, B.A. *R* | | X | |
| **ST. LUCY** | | | |
|   J. Brathwaite, M.A. *R* | | X | |
|   J.P. Wall *A/C* | X | | |
| **ST. ANDREW** | | | |
|   J.G. Lewis *R* | | X | |
| **ST. JOSEPH** | | | |
|   H. Parkinson *R* | | X | |

The Mother Country seems to have been responsible for 9 assistant curates, the Bishop, the Archdeacon, the Garrison Chaplain and possibly the Bishop's Chaplain.

The Colony was responsible for 11 rectors and 3½ assistant curates.

Codrington Trust Estates was responsible for 3½ staff at Codrington College and Codrington School.

*Note*: '½' represents a shared responsibility, and not necessarily 50 per cent of stipend.

## Pay for Teachers and Catechists

A list of stipends for teachers and catechists for the quarter ended 6/7/1839.

(K) gives annual rates for (in Barbados):

(a) 32 teachers from £50 to £20 (majority £30) from the 'Mixed Fund'.
(b) Lay readers/catechists Mr. Morle £100 from HM Treasury.
(c) Mr. C.A. Newsam (later a student at Codrington College and A/C at St. Andrew's 1841) £100 from SPG.
(d) 7 male teachers at £25 and 1 female at £15 from the Christian Faith Society.

The Diocese's total for the year (calculated on the basis of this quarter) was:

| | |
|---|---|
| Mixed Fund | £2,887 |
| HM Treasury | £700 |
| SPG | £390 |
| SPCK | £105 |
| Christian Faith Society | £700 |
| Total | £4,782 sterling |

# APPENDIX III

## Coleridge: Builder and Rebuilder

| Built during the Episcopate of William Harte Coleridge | |
|---|---|
| ST. JUDE<br>HOLY INNOCENTS<br>ST. ALBANS – C/S<br>ST. CLEMENT<br>ST. SWITHIN<br>ST. SAVIOUR<br>ST. SIMON-C/S<br>ST. JOSEPH'S – C/S<br>ST. CATHERINE – C/S<br>ST. MARTIN – C/S<br>ST. DAVID – C/S<br>ST. LAWRENCE<br>ST. MATTHIAS<br>ST. BARNABAS<br>ST. STEPHEN<br>ST. GILES – C/S<br>ST. MARY | * – Parish Church<br>C/S – Chapel-School<br>All others are Chapels of Ease |
| ST. LUKE<br>ST. MARK<br>HOLY TRINITY<br>ST. BARTHOLOMEW<br>ST. MATTHEW<br>ST. PAUL | Places of worship rebuilt after the hurricane of 1831 |

**BUILT BEFORE 1824**

ALL SAINTS
CODRINGTON ESTATE CHAPEL
ST. THOMAS*
ST. PETER*
ST. LUCY*
ST. JOSEPH*
ST. JOHN*
ST. PHILIP*
CHRIST CHURCH*
ST. GEORGE*
ST. JAMES*
ST. ANDREW*
ST. MICHAEL*
CODRINGTON COLLEGE CHAPEL

| CHURCH | Built | Rebuilt | Cost in £ | Accommodation | Worshippers | Communicants |
|---|---|---|---|---|---|---|
| **GROUP 1 – In existence in 1824 and not rebuilt (hurricane repairs in brackets)** | | | | | | |
| *ST. MICHAEL | | | (1,563) | 1,700 | 1,000 | 260 |
| CODRINGTON COLLEGE CHAPEL | | | | 46 | 40 | 29 |
| *ST. ANDREW | | | (615) | 700 | 800 | 56 |
| *ST. JAMES | | | (325) | 550 | 360 | 65 |
| *ST. GEORGE | | | (682) | 900 | 830 | 120 |
| **GROUP II – REBUILT** | | | | | | |
| *CHRIST CHURCH | 1837 | | 6,000 | 1,300 | 1,000 | 150 |
| *ST. PHILIP | 1836 | | 6,000 | 1,200 | 900 | 165 |
| *ST. JOHN | 1836 | | 6,000 | 1,200 | 1,000 | 164 |
| CODRINGTON ESTATE CHAPEL | 1833 | | 1,800 | 800 | 900 | 100 |
| *ST. JOSEPH | 1839 | | 2,625 | 800 | 750 | 125 |
| *ST. LUCY | 1837 | | 4,500 | 1,200 | 800 | 120 |
| *ST. PETER | 1837 | | 4,620 | 1,000 | 900 | 16 |
| ALL SAINTS | 1841† | | | | | |
| *ST. THOMAS | 1837 | | 4,000 | 810 | 800 | 90 |
| **GROUP III – NEW BUILDINGS** | | | | | | |
| ST. MARY | 1827 | | 13,000 | 1,420 | 1,200 | 250 |
| ST. PAUL | 1831 | 1832 | 3,000 | 1,200 | 1,200 | 330 |
| ST. MATTHEW | 1829 | 1832 | 850 | 580 | 600 | 40 |
| ST. GILES – C/S | 1836 | | 500 | 275 | 200 | N/A |
| ST. STEPHEN | 1836 | | 1,300 | 530 | 490 | 70 |
| ST. BARNABAS – C/S | 1838 | | 1,200 | 500 | 450 | 30 |
| ST. BARTHOLOMEW | 1831 | 1832 | 900 | 540 | 500 | 75 |
| ST. MATTHIAS | 1841† | | | **270 | 200 | N/A |
| ST. LAWRENCE – C/S | 1837 | | 550 | 175 | 200 | 40 |
| ST. DAVID-C/S | 1840 | | 975 | 400 | 380 | 30 |
| HOLY TRINITY | 1829 | 1832 | 1087 | 500 | 420 | 70 |
| ST. MARTIN-C/S | 1837 | | 525 | 300 | 300 | N/A |
| ST. CATHERINE – C/S | 1841 | | 375 | | | |
| ST. MARK | ?1831 | 1832 | 855 | 360 | 340 | 83 |
| ST. JOSEPH'S – C/S | 1837 | | 300 | 200 | 120 | N/A |
| ST. SIMON-C/S | 1840 | | 562 | 290 | 320 | 14 |
| ST. SAVIOUR | 1841† | | | **500 | 500 | N/A |
| ST. SWITHIN | 1841† | | | | | |
| ST. CLEMENT | 1838 | | 400 | 300 | 260 | 45 |
| ST. ALBANS – C/S | 1840 | 1832 | 500 | 176 | 150 | N/A |
| HOLY INNOCENTS | 1838 | | 2,000 | 500 | 450 | 25 |
| ST. LUKE | 1832 | | 750 | 700 | 475 | 70 |
| ST. JUDE | 1834 | | 1,170 | 400 | 400 | 75 |

\* – Parish Church   C/S – Chapel-School   † – In process of building   ** – In temporary place of worship

# NOTES

## CHAPTER 1

1. C.F. Pascoe, *Classified Digest of the Records of the Society for the Propagation of the Gospel in Foreign Parts 1701–1892* (London, 1894), pp. 194, 200.
2. A. Caldecott, *The Church in the West Indies* (Frank Cass, 1970), p. 49.
3. W.W. Manross, *A History of the American Episcopal Church*, (N.Y.: Morehouse-Gorham Co., 1959), pp. 41–42.
4. Ibid., p. 43.
5. W.W. Manross, op. cit., pp. 44–45.
6. Ibid., p. 45.
7. Ibid., pp. 45–46.
8. Ibid., p. 46.
9. The Lucas Manuscript: 'The Commission of Surrogate of the Bishop of London in Barbados', *Journal of the Barbados Museum and Historical Society*, Vol. XV, No. 4, 174; see also Lucas MS, Vol. 2, 3, 15 July 1718, Barbados Museum and Historical Society (hereafter cited as BMHS), 35.
10. Caldecott, op. cit., pp. 51–52; see also Lucas MS. Vol. XV, no. 4, 188.
11. Lucas MS, Vol. 2, 3, BMHS, 35–36.
12. Lucas MS, loc. cit., Vol. XV, no. 4, 175.
13. Ibid., 176.
14. Ibid., 176–79.
15. Hall's Laws, BMHS, 241–42.
16. Pascoe, op. cit., footnote p. 227.
17. *Fulham Papers*, Vol. 2, BMHS, 647.
18. L.J. Ragatz, *The Fall of the Planter Class in the British Caribbean 1763–1833* (Octagon, 1971), pp. 404, 406ff.
19. The Society was the Trustee of these Estates since 1710, as a result of Christopher Codrington's bequest with which we shall deal in Ch. 3.

20. J.H. Bennett, Jr., *Bondsmen and Bishop: Slavery and Apprenticeship on the Codrington Plantations of Barbados, 1710–1838* (California, 1958), pp. 100–111.
21. Pascoe, op. cit., p. 114.
22. Ragatz, op. cit., pp. 414–15.
23. Caldecott, op. cit., pp. 89ff.

# CHAPTER 2

1. L. Stephen (ed.), *Dictionary of National Biography*, Vol. XI (Smith, Edler & Co., 1886), pp. 317–18.
2. Christ Church Archives, X.C 297, Oxford, gives the date of entry as 15 January; J. Foster (ed.), *Alumni Oxoniensis 1715–1886,* Vol. 1 (London), p. 278. Foster gives 28 January as the date of matriculation.
3. Ibid.
4. *Historical Register of the University of Oxford* (Oxford, 1900), p. 641.
5. L. Stephen (ed.), op. cit., p. 318 (see also J. Foster, op. cit.).
6. Ibid.
7. Letter from the Bishop of London to Coleridge (Private), Downing Street, 23 January 1824.
8. C.F. Pascoe, *Two Hundred Years of SPG,* p. 200.
9. British Guiana was added to the Diocese of Barbados by Letters Patent in 1826 (see C.F. Pascoe, ibid., footnote). See also 'Annexation of British Guiana to the Diocese', *Ecclesiastical Calendar of the Diocese of Barbados and the Leeward Islands* (Bridgetown, Barbados, 1839). Bodleian, pp. 1–5.
10. Letters Patent creating the Diocese of Barbados in 1824 – George IV, BMHS.
11. *Bishop's Document Book, 1824–1849,* Barbados Department of Archives, p. 1.
12. Letter to Bishop from I.W. Horton, 16 November 1824, under instructions from Lord Bathurst, *Bishop's Document Book,* p. 2.
13. A. Caldecott, *The Church in the West Indies,* p. 91.
14. Letter to the Bishop of London from Earl Liverpool, Fife House, 21 June 1824. Bishop's private collection of letters. The Bishop noted on 30 September 1825 that a copy was sent to the Colonial Office.
15. *The Barbadian,* 28 January 1825, BMHS. It should be observed that there was no 'Lady' with Bishop Coleridge on his arrival in Barbados. In 1825 he married the eldest daughter of Dr. Thomas Rennell, Dean of Winchester and Master of the Temple. She was also granddaughter of Sir William Blackstone,

Judge. To them were born a son and a daughter (see L. Stephen, op. cit., p. 318).
16. *The Barbadian,* 1 February 1825, BMHS (see also a Letter from Bishop Coleridge to the Right Honourable Earl Bathurst, 'Gibraltar', Barbados, 11 February 1825).
17. Ibid.
18. Ibid.
19. *The Barbadian,* 14 February 1825, BMHS.
20. Letter from Bishop Coleridge to Earl Bathurst, 11 February 1825.
21. Extracts from a Notebook of the Rt. Rev. W.H. Coleridge, Bishop of Barbados, on his First Tour of his Diocese 1825 (Warren Alleyne Collection, Barbados), p. 11.
22. Ibid., p. 9.
23. Ibid., p. 10.
24. Circular to Governor administering His Majesty's Island of —— re authority to collate clergymen to vacant benefices. Downing Street, 30 June, Earl Bathurst, Bishop's Document Book, p. 26.
25. Letter to Bishop from Downing Street, 10 January 1826, in reply to Bishop's letter of 21 December. I.W. Horton, *Bishop's Document Book,* p. 31.
26. Circular to Governors. Downing Street, 29 June 1828. G. Murray, ibid.
27. Letter to Bishop from Downing Street, 14 February 1829. G. Murray, ibid., pp. 31–33.

## CHAPTER 3

1. Extracts from the Bishop's Notebook (Warren Alleyne Collection, Barbados), pp. 1, 6.
2. 'Diocese of Barbados and the Leeward Islands, instituted 1824, Archdeaconry and Rural Deanery of Barbados', *Table of Returns 1841,* USPG Archives, London.
3. Appendix to Letter from Bishop Coleridge to Earl Bathurst (Secretary for War and the Colonies 1812–1827), 9 December 1825.
4. Coleridge to Bathurst, and Memorial of the Church Building Committee in Barbados to the Lords Commissioners of H.M. Treasury, 4 May 1825, CO 28/146, Public Record Office (PRO) 7096.
5. Extracts, p. 5.
6. Copy of Treasury Minute, 6 October 1826, CO 28/146, PRO X/K 1520.

7. 'Diocese of Barbados and the Leeward Islands', *Table of Returns 1841*, and *Statements of Funds 1837*, USPG Archives. See also Appendix I.
8. *Extracts*, p. 5.
9. S.S. Goodridge, *St. Mary's 1827–1977* (Caribbean Graphic Production, Barbados, 1977).
10. *Extracts*, p. 8.
11. See Appendix I for a summary statement of funds.
12. Ibid.
13. Ibid.
14. 'A Letter addressed to His Excellency Major-General Sir Lionel Smith, K.C.B., relative to the distribution of the Parliamentary Grant for the Relief of the Sufferers from the Hurricane of August 11, 1831', 22 July 1833, *Sermons and Tracts*, G. Pamph. 2696, Bodleian, Oxford, p. 6.
15. Ibid.
16. Ibid.
17. See Appendix I.
18. Ibid.
19. 'A Charge addressed to the Clergy of the Diocese of Barbados and the Leeward Islands, 1834', W.H. Coleridge, in *Charges and Addresses* (London: J.G. & F. Rivington, 1836), BMHS, pp. 176–77.
20. B. Hill, 'The Coleridge Chapels of Ease', *Journal of the Barbados Museum and Historical Society*, Vol. XXXVI, No. 1 (1979), 16–27.
21. Ibid. See also, 'A Charge . . . 1834', loc. cit., p. 153.
22. 'Laying of Corner-Stone of St. Barnabas Chapel School in the Parish of St. Michael in the Island of Barbados', Extract from *The Barbadian*, 'Miscellanea', in *Sermons and Tracts*, p. 50.
23. *The Barbadian*, 18 February 1825.
24. Ibid., 8 March 1825.
25. Ibid., 11 March 1825.
26. Ibid., 18 March 1825.
27. Letter to Bishop from W. Garnett, Bridgetown, 26 February 1825, *Bishop's Document Book*, pp. 13–16.
28. *Extracts*, p. 6.
29. 'Replies to Questions Addressed to the Clergy of the Diocese of Barbados and the Leeward Islands, up to December 31, 1828', USPG Archives.
30. 'A Charge . . . 1834', loc. cit., pp. 175–76.
31. S. Lushington, 'Pews in Parish Churches', October 9, 1837, 'Miscellanea', loc. cit., pp. 23–24.
32. Extract from the *Oxford Herald*, 'Miscellanea', loc. cit., pp. 24–25.

33. 'Acts for Exchange of Glebe in the Parish of St. Thomas and to Prevent the Holding of Elections, etc., in the Parish Churches', *The Barbadian*, 21 March 1838.
34. 'Diocese of Barbados and the Leeward Islands', *Table of Returns 1841*. See also Appendix III.
35. 'Laying of the Corner-Stone of St. Barnabas Chapel School', loc. cit.

# CHAPTER 4

1. Letter from W.H. Coleridge to the Rev. John Keble, 11 February 1824, in '4 Letters from W.H. Coleridge to the Rev. John Keble, Oriel College, 1823–1846', The Archives, Keble College, Oxford, p. 142.
2. Keble to John Taylor Coleridge, 2 March 1824, in 'Letters from John Keble to John Taylor Coleridge', Vol. I, 1811–39, MS. Eng. Lett. d. 134, Bodleian, p. 156. John Taylor Coleridge was Bishop Coleridge's cousin. John Keble, scholar, distinguished churchman and Catholic Revivalist, was a close friend and mentor of the Coleridge family at Ottery St. Mary, Devon.
3. Keble to John Taylor Coleridge, 22 February 1826; 22 January 1827; 1 December 1831, ibid., pp. 182, 193, 235.
4. Keble to John Taylor Coleridge, October 1833 and 3 December 1834, ibid., p. 235. See also Coleridge to Keble, 30 December 1834 in '4 Letters from W.H. Coleridge'.
5. Letter from Downing Street, 16 November 1824, 'Temporalia, or Instructions for the Clergy, relative to Ordination, Institution to Archdeaconries, and Benefices, Drawing for Salaries, Granting of Licences etc. etc. in the Diocese of Barbados and the Leeward Islands', in *Sermons and Tracts*, pp. 17–18.
6. Letter from Downing Street, 18 November 1824, ibid.
7. 'Archdeacons' Patent, Bathurst 1825', 'Ecclesiastical Calendar of the Diocese of Barbados and the Leeward Islands, Bridgeham 1839', 'Miscellanea', in *Sermons and Tracts*, pp. 6–8.
8. See List of Signatures to an Address to the Governor of British Guiana, His Excellency Henry Light, 'Miscellanea', in *Sermons and Tracts*, pp. 30–31.
9. 'Circular Relative to Office etc. of Rural Deans', Appendix A to 'A Letter addressed to the Clergy of the Diocese on the Bishop's Return from England in 1829', Coleridge, *Charges and Addresses*, pp. 55–59.
10. Document Book, p. 86.
11. 'List of Clergy, 1 January 1839, Diocese of Barbados and the Leeward Islands', 'Miscellanea', in *Sermons and Tracts*, p. 67.

12. 'Comparative Statement of the Number of Clergy and of Charity Schools in the years 1812, 1825, 1834, in the Diocese of Barbados', 'Appendix', Coleridge, *Charges and Addresses*. See also R.H. Schomburgk, *The History of Barbados*. (London: Longman, 1847), p. 99. From the list of clergy appointed to preach at the Parish Church of St. Michael on Wednesdays and Fridays during Lent, as recorded by *The Barbadian*, 11 February 1825, we learn the names of the majority of the clergy: the Rev. William Garnett (Rector of St. Michael); the Rev. T.H. Orderson (R. of Christ Church); the Rev. J.F. Pilgrim (R. of St. James); the Rev. W.M. Payne (R. of St. Andrew); the Rev. W.M. Harte (R. of St. Lucy); the Rev. W. Als (R. of St. Philip); the Rev. W.L. Pinder (R. of St. George); the Rev. G.F. Maynard (R. of St. Thomas); the Rev. J.H. Gittens (R. of St. John); the Rev. W.P. Hinds (R. of St. Joseph); the Rev. H. Parkinson (Acting Principal of Codrington College); the Rev. John Packer (Master of the Central School); the Rev. R.F. King (Lecturer, St. Michael's). We have already mentioned that the Chaplain on the Codrington Estates was the Rev. J.H. Pinder.
13. Extracts, p. 6.
14. J.E. Reece and C.G. Clark-Hunt, *Barbados Diocesan History*, (London: The West India Committee, 1925), p. 99.
15. For a full account see J.T. Gilmore, 'The Rev. William Harte and Attitudes to Slavery in Early Nineteenth-Century Barbados', *Journal of Ecclesiastical History*, Vol. 30, No. 4 (Cambridge, October 1979), pp. 461–74. See also Goodridge, *St. Mary's 1827–1877*, pp. 12–13, 32; and Schomburgk, op. cit., pp. 427–29.
16. Bennett, Jr., *Bondsmen and Bishop*, p. 116.
17. Gilmore, loc. cit., pp. 466–67.
18. 'Opinion of Dr. Lushington, Doctors Commons, 5 November 1824', 'Temporalia', in *Sermons and Tracts*, pp. 2–4.
19. *Christian Remembrancer*, XI, 1829, British Museum, 49.
20. 'List of Clergy ordained within the Diocese of Barbados and the Leeward Islands', Appendix to 'Address privately delivered to Candidates for the Holy Order of Priests on 27 June 1835, previous to their ordination on 29 June 1835', in *Sermons and Tracts*, pp. 9 ff.
21. Ibid. A full list of Ordinations up to 1835 is given.
22. J. Foster, *Alumni Oxonienses 1500–1714*, Vol. I, p. 297.
23. Quoted in Bennett, Jr., op. cit., p. 1.
24. T.H. Bindley, *Annals of Codrington College Barbados*, (London: The West India Committee, 1911), p. 28.

25. Quoted, ibid., pp. 31–32.
26. Ibid., p. 32.
27. 'A Letter Addressed to the Clergy of the Diocese on the Bishop's Return from England in 1829', Coleridge, *Charges and Addresses*, pp. 37–41.
28. Schomburgk, op. cit., p. 118; F.J. Klingberg, *Codrington Chronicle* (California, 1949), p. 120; Bindley, op cit., p. 32.
29  *The Barbadian*, 10 September 1830, BMHS. See also *SPCK Report 1831*, SPCK Archives, 51; and Bindley, op. cit., p. 33. The date, 12 October 1830, given by C.F. Pascoe, *Two Hundred Years of SPG*, p. 782, refers to the beginning of term.
30. *The Barbadian*, 10 September 1830.
31. Ibid.
32. Ibid. See also Bindley, op. cit., p. 33; and Schomburgk, op. cit., p. 119.
33. 'Letter from Coleridge to SPG', 25 September 1830, Barbados (Diocesan) 1824–1846, USPG Archives. See also Bindley, op. cit., pp. 33, 57. From Bindley's list we see that some of the Exhibitioners and Commoners were Foundation Scholars.
34. 'Letter from Coleridge to SPG', 25 September 1830, loc. cit.
35. *SPCK Report 1831*, loc. cit.
36. 'Minutes [in hand of Hawkins] of a meeting at 79 Pall Mall, 9 August 1842, attended by Archdeacons Parry, Davis and Austin', Barbados (Diocesan) 1824–1846, p. 261.
37. Bindley, op. cit., pp. 33, 57.
38. Ibid., p. 34.
39. 'List of Clergy Ordained', loc. cit.
40. 'A Charge . . . 1834', Coleridge, *Charges and Addresses*, p. 154.
41. 'List of Clergy Ordained', loc. cit.
42. Bindley, op. cit., p. 34.
43. Ibid., pp. 57–58.
44. 'List of Clergy, 1 January 1839, Diocese of Barbados and the Leeward Islands', 'Miscellanea', in *Sermons and Tracts*, p. 67 ff.
45. Schomburgk, op. cit., pp. 119–20.
46. 'Report of W.W. Jackson, Reader at Claybury estate in the Parish of St. John, 3 May 1831', Barbados (Diocesan) 1824–1846, pp. 56–59.
47. 'A Charge . . . 1834', loc. cit., pp. 155–58.
48. Bennett, Jr., op. cit., pp. 75–110.
49. *SPCK Report 1826*, loc. cit., p. 31.
50. Extracts, p. 7ff.

51. A. Caldecott, *Church in the West Indies*, p. 105.
52. 'Appendix B' after 'Sermon preached by Archdeacon Edward Eliot, B.D., in the Cathedral, 11 February 1827', *Sermons and Tracts*, op. cit., p. 33.
53. 'A Charge ... 1834', loc. cit., pp. 155–59.
54. 'Letter from W.D. Sealy, Rector of St. Peter's to John H. Gittens, Rural Dean, 1 June 1835', Barbados (Diocesan) 1824–1846, p. 75.
55. 'Letter from Treasury, T. Chambers', 20 September 1824, 'Salaries, Licences of Absence etc. etc.', in *Sermons and Tracts*, p. 21.
56. 7 Georgii 4. Cap. 4, ibid., pp. 21–22.
57. Coleridge to Bathurst, 4 May 1825, CO 28/146, PRO, 7096.
58. 'A Primary Charge 1830', Coleridge, *Charges and Addresses*, p. 69 ff.
59. Schomburgk, op. cit., p. 102.
60. 'Stipend List for Quarter ending October 10, 1838', Barbados (Diocesan) 1824–1846.
61. Ibid.
62. 'Replies to Bishop's Circular re information from Parishes, addressed to John H. Gittens, Rural Dean, 1835', Barbados (Diocesan) 1824–1846, p. 68ff.
63. 'Stipend List ... 1838', loc. cit. See also Appendix II.
64. 'Letter from Downing Street, 19 November 1829', 'Salaries, Licences of Absence', op. cit., p. 22.
65. 'Letter from Downing Street, 22 October 1832', ibid., p. 23.
66. 'Letter from Downing Street, 15 October 1835', ibid., p. 24.
67. 'A Charge to the Clergy in British Guiana', 23 March 1836, 'Miscellanea', in *Sermons and Tracts*, pp. 10–11.
68. 'The Society for the Relief of the Widows and Fatherless Children of Clergymen in the Diocese of Barbados and the Leeward Islands, meeting in 1839', 'Miscellanea', in *Sermons and Tracts*, p. 59 ff.
69. 'Letter from W.G. Grant, Island Secretary, Spanish Town, Jamaica, to W.H. Coleridge, 21 November 1839, with copy of a Resolution of Council', Barbados (Diocesan) 1824–1846, pp. 200–201.
70. 'Coleridge to Keble, 30 December 1834', in '4 Letters from W.H. Coleridge'.

## CHAPTER 5

1. Extracts from the Bishop's Notebook, pp. 1–2.
2. Ibid., p. 4.
3. Ibid., p. 2.
4. F.A. Hoyos, *Barbados, A History from the Amerindians to Independence* (London: Macmillan, 1978), pp. 140, 142.

5. Extracts, pp. 2–3.
6. R.H. Schomburgk, *The History of Barbados*, p. 105.
7. Extracts, p. 3.
8. Ibid.
9. *SPCK Report 1828*, SPCK Archives London, p. 49.
10. Extracts, p. 4.
11. Ibid.
12. Ibid.
13. 'School for the Education of the Poor White Children of the Parish of St. Peter's, Barbados', *The Christian Remembrancer*, Vol. X (1828), British Museum, pp. 717–18.
14. Extracts, p.5.
15. 'A Primary Charge 1830', W.H. Coleridge, *Charges and Addresses*, p. 103.
16. Extracts, p. 2.
17. Ibid., pp. 2–3. See also *SPCK Report 1826*, SPCK Archives, pp. 30–31.
18. Extracts, p. 2.
19. Ibid.
20. 'Some Facts Relating to the Present State of the Slave-Population in Certain Parts of the West Indies', *The Christian Remembrancer*, Vol. VI (1828), p. 773.
21. Extracts, p. 4.
22. *SPCK Report 1821*, SPCK Archives, p. 116.
23. Reece and Clark-Hunt, *Barbados Diocesan History*, pp. 69–70.
24. *SPCK Report 1826*, pp. 30–31.
25. *SPCK Report 1828*, p. 50.
26. Ibid.
27. *SPCK Report 1829*, p. 44.
28. 'Extract from the Report of the Barbados Diocesan Committee of the Society for Promoting Christian Knowledge for its Thirteenth Year', 'Miscellanea', in *Sermons and Tracts*, pp. 39–40.
29. *The Christian Remembrancer*, Vol. VI, p. 774.
30. Schomburgk, op. cit., pp. 106, 131.
31. *SPCK Report 1827*, p. 39.
32. *SPCK Report 1828*, p. 49.
33. *SPCK Report 1829*, p. 44.
34. 'Address to Candidates for Holy Orders' 1828, Coleridge, *Charges and Addresses*, pp. 27–28.
35. 'A Letter addressed to the Clergy of the Diocese on the Bishop's Return from England in 1829', ibid., pp. 42–46.

36. 'A Primary Charge 1830', ibid., pp. 71–72.
37. Ibid., pp. 91–92.
38. Copy of Circular, Downing Street, 16 November 1835, Glenelg, *Document Book,* The Department of Archives, Barbados, p. 80.
39. Circular from Glenelg, 25 November 1835, ibid.
40. Copy of Circular from George Grey, Downing Street, 21 July 1835, ibid., p. 81.
41. 'The Reverend John Sterling's Report 1835', S. Gordon, *Reports and Repercussions in West Indian Education 1835–1933* (Ginn & Co. Ltd., 1968), pp. 60–66.
42. *Document Book,* p. 81.
43. Ibid.
44. Copy of Circular from George Grey, Downing Street, September 1835, ibid., p. 82.
45. Ibid.
46. 'Replies to Bishop's Circular re information from Parishes, addressed to John H. Gittens, Rural Dean, 1835', Barbados (Diocesan) 1824–1846, pp. 68 ff.
47. Ibid.
48. Ibid.
49. 'Schools, in Connexion with the Church, for the Religious Instruction of the Poor', 1825–1834, 'Appendix', Coleridge, *Charges and Addresses.*
50. 'Schools in Barbados, in Connexion with the Church, for the Religious Instruction of the Poor', 31 December 1838, 'Miscellanea', in *Sermons and Tracts,* p. 75 ff.
51. 'A List of Salaries of Teachers from the Mixed Fund, HM. Treasury, SPG, SPCK and Christian Faith Society for the Quarter ending 6 July, 1839', Barbados (Diocesan) 1824–1846, pp. 196–99.
52. Hoyos, op. cit., p. 143; Schomburgk, op. cit., p. 106.
53. Schomburgk, op. cit., pp. 118–19.
54. T.H. Bindley, *Annals of Codrington College Barbados,* p. 38.

## CHAPTER 6

1. 'An Address privately delivered to Candidates for the Holy Order of Priests on 27 June 1835, previously to their Ordination on 29 June 1835', *Sermons and Tracts,* 8, pp. 1–4.
2. 'An Address in the Cathedral and Parish Church of Saint Michael at an Ordination of Deacons, 6 January 1836', ibid., 9, p. 45.

3. 'A Charge delivered to the Clergy of the Church of England in British Guiana. 23 March 1836', ibid., 10, p. 4.
4. 'A Charge addressed to the Clergy of the Diocese of Barbados and the Leeward Islands 1834', W.H. Coleridge, *Charges and Addresses*, pp. 149, 184–85.
5. 'An Address in the Cathedral . . . 6 January 1836', op. cit., pp. 16–17.
6. 'An Address privately delivered to candidates for the Holy Order of Deacons, on the day previous to their Ordination, May 27, 1835', *Sermons and Tracts*, 7, pp. 11, 14–16. See also 'Address . . . 27 June 1835', ibid., p. 9.
7. 'An Address . . . 27 May 1835', ibid., p. 17.
8. 'A Primary Charge . . . 1830', W.H. Coleridge, *Charges and Addresses*, pp. 106–7.
9. 'An Address . . . May 27, 1835', op. cit., p. 10. See also 'An Address . . . 6 January 1836', op. cit., p. 23.
10. 'An Address to Candidates for Holy Orders 1828', W.H. Coleridge, *Charges and Addresses*, pp. 25–27.
11. 'A Letter Addressed to the Clergy of the Diocese on the Bishop's Return from England in 1829', ibid., p. 43
12. 'An Address . . . 6 January 1836', op. cit., p. 25.
13. 'Extract from a Sermon preached by the Bishop in the Parish Church of SI. John's, in the Island of Barbados on the occasion of the Consolidation of the Parochial Schools of that Parish, in 1827', W.H. Coleridge, *Charges and Addresses*, pp. 116–17.
14. Ibid., pp. 118–19.
15. Mentioned in the General Appendix, W.H. Coleridge, *Charges and Addresses*
16. 'A Letter addressed to the Clergy . . . on Bishop's return from England in 1829', op. cit., pp. 43–46.
17. 'An Address . . . 6 January 1836', op. cit., pp. 25–26.
18. 'An Address to Candidates for Holy Orders 1828', op. cit., pp. 21–24.
19. 'A Letter addressed to the Clergy . . . in 1829', op. cit., p. 52.
20. 'An Address to Candidates for Holy Orders 1828', op. cit., p. 6.
21. Ibid., pp. 13–20. See also 'A Second Address to Candidates for Holy Orders 1832', W.H. Coleridge, *Charges and Addresses* etc., p. 136.
22. 'An Address privately delivered to candidates for the Holy Order of Deacons, May 27, 1835', op. cit., p. 9.
23. 'A Primary Charge . . . 1830', op. cit., 89–90.
24. 'A Charge . . . 1834', ibid., p. 188.
25. 'A Primary Charge . . . 1830', ibid., pp. 101–3. See also 'A Charge . . . 1834', ibid., p. 179.

26. *A Selection of Psalms and Hymns from the Authorized metrical versions of the Psalms of David and from the annexed to the Book of Common Prayer, with appropriate tunes. Recommended for the use of the Cathedral and other Churches of the Diocese of Barbados and the Leeward Islands* (Bridgetown, The Barbadian Office, 1831). British Museum.
27. J.H. Bennett, Jr., *Bondsmen and Bishop*, pp. 22-23, 80-81.
28. J.T. Gilmore, 'The Rev. William Harte and Attitudes to Slavery in Early Nineteenth-Century Barbados', *Journal of Ecclesiastical History,* Vol. 30, No. 4, October 1979, 467.
29. Ibid., p. 72.
30. 'Extract from a Sermon preached by the Bishop in the Parish of St. John's, 1827', op. cit., pp. 113-14.
31. *SPCK Report 1828*, SPCK Archives, 50. See also *The Christian Remembrancer*, Vol. VI, 1828, 772.
32. 'A Primary Charge . . . 1830', op. cit., p. 68.
33. 'A Charge . . . 1834', ibid., p. 151.
34. Ibid.
35. 'An Address . . . 6 January 1836', op. cit., p. 27.
36. 'A Second Address . . . 1832'; 'A Charge . . . 1834', op. cit., pp. 138, 161-62.
37. ' A Charge . . . 1834', ibid., pp. 163-64.
38. Ibid., pp. 164-65.
39. 'A Primary Charge . . . 1830', ibid., p. 71.
40. Ibid., pp. 93-95.
41. A Charge... 1834', ibid., pp. 165-66.
42. 'A Second Address . . . 1832', ibid., p. 139.
43. 'A Charge . . . 1834', ibid., pp. 166-68.
44. 'A Primary Charge . . . 1830', ibid., p. 96.
45. 'A Letter addressed to the Clergy . . . 1829', ibid., pp. 47-51.
46. Bennett, Jr., op. cit., p. 35.
47. Ibid., pp. 117-22.
48. Ibid., pp. 122-23.
49. *SPCK Report 1836*, SPCK Archives, 66.
50. 'A Charge . . . 1834', op. cit., pp. 172-73.
51. *SPCK Report 1835*, SPCK Archives, 67.
52. Circular from the Bishop to the Clergy, 24 February 1825, *Document Book*, p. 3.
53. 'A Primary Charge . . . 1830', op. cit., 97.
54. Circular from the Bishop to the Clergy, 1830, *Document Book*, p. 97.

55. Appendix B to 'A Charge ... 1834', op. cit., p. 194.
56. 'A Charge ... 1834', ibid., pp. 170–71.
57. Ibid., pp. 173–74.
58. 'A Primary Charge ... 1830', ibid., pp. 70–71.
59. Ibid.
60. *Document Book,* pp. 19–25.
61. 'A Primary Charge ... 1830', op. cit., pp. 97, 100.
62. 'An Address ... May 27, 1835', op. cit., pp. 18–19.

# CHAPTER 7

1. J.H. Bennett, Jr., *Bondsmen and Bishop,* p. 125.
2. Ibid., p. 126.
3. Ibid., p. 127.
4. Ibid., pp. 127–29.
5. Ibid., pp. 129–30.
6. R.H. Schomburgk, *The History of Barbados,* p. 460; F.A. Hoyos, *Barbados, A History,* p. 126.
7. Hoyos, ibid., p. 127.
8. Ibid., p. 121.
9. Ibid., p. 126.
10. Bennett, Jr., op. cit., p. 131.
11. Ibid., p. 132.
12. Ibid., p. 133.
13. Ibid.
14. Schomburgk, op. cit., p. 483 ff.; Hoyos, op. cit., pp. 129–30.
15. Bennett, Jr., op. cit., p. 134.
16. 'Termination of the Apprenticeships on the Trust Estates in the Island of Barbados, Belonging to the "Society for the Propagation of the Gospel in Foreign Parts"', 'Miscellanea', in *Sermons and Tracts,* p. 47.
17. Ibid., pp. 47–48.
18. Ibid., pp. 48–49.
19. Ibid., p. 49.
20. Bennett, Jr., op. cit., p. 135; Hoyos, op. cit., p. 130.
21. Bennett, Jr., ibid., pp. 128–29.
22. A. Caldecott, *The Church in the West Indies,* p. 114.
23. *SPCK Report 1837,* SPCK Archives, p. 81.
24. Caldecott, op. cit., p. 114; Schomburgk, op. cit., p. 128.

25. *The Barbadian,* 16 December 1835.
26. A full list of these institutions is given in the General Appendix to W.H. Coleridge, *Charges and Addresses.* See also L. Stephen (ed.), *Dictionary of National Biography,* p. 318.
27. Quoted by C.F. Pascoe, *Two Hundred Years of the SPG,* p. 203.

## CHAPTER 8

1. F.G. Coleridge to John Keble, 'Coleridge Letters' (R131–142), 134, The Archives, Keble College, Oxford.
2. Coleridge to Keble, Salston House, 4 May 1846, '4 Letters from W.H. Coleridge to Rev. John Keble', ibid., 142.
3. *A Sermon preached in the Abbey Church, Westminster ... at the Consecration of ... Thomas, Lord Bishop of Barbados, George, Lord Bishop of Gibraltar, Francis Russell, Lord Bishop of Tasmania, Daniel Gateward, Lord Bishop of Antigua, William Piercy, Lord Bishop of Guiana* (London: F.G.F. & J. Rivington, 1842). British Museum.
4. *A Sermon preached in the Chapel of Lambeth Palace, at the Consecration of the Lord Bishop of New Zealand* (London: F.G.F. & J. Rivington, 1841). British Museum.
5. Edward Coleridge to John Keble, 12 August 1843, '19 Letters from Edward Coleridge to John Keble', Coleridge Letters, 132.
6. Ibid.
7. C.F. Pascoe, *Two Hundred Years of the SPG,* pp. 796–97.
8. Reference to T.G. Marshall, 'The Folk Song in Barbadian Society' (1976, Unpublished Monograph, 1) in F.A. Hoyos, *Barbados, A History* p. 122.

# BIBLIOGRAPHY

## BOOKS

Bennett, J.H., Jr. *Bondsmen and Bishop: Slavery and Apprenticeship on the Codrington Plantations of Barbados, 1710–1838*. California, 1958.
Bindley, T.H. *Annals of Codrington College Barbados*. London: The West India Committee, 1911.
Caldecott, A. *The Church in the West Indies*. Frank Cass, 1970.
Coleridge, W.H. *Charges and Addresses*, ... London: I.G.Y.F. Rivington, 1836.
Foster, J. (ed.). *Alumni Oxoniensis 1500–1714*, Vol. 1. London.
——. *Alumni Oxoniensjs 1715–1886*, Vol. 2. London.
Goodridge, S.S. *St. Mary's 1827–1977*. Barbados: Caribbean Graphic Production, 1977.
Gordon, S. *Reports and Repercussions in West Indian Education 1835–1933*. Boston: Ginn and Co. Ltd., 1968.
Hoyos, F.A. *Barbados: A History from the Amerindians to Independence*. London: Macmillan, 1978.
Klingberg, F. J. *Codrington Chronicle*. California, 1949.
Manross, W.W. *A History of the American Episcopal Church*. New York: Morehouse-Gorham Co., 1959.
Pascoe, C.F. *Two Hundred Years of SPG: Classified Digest of the Records of the Society for the Propagation of the Gospel in Foreign Parts 1701–1892*. London, 1894.
Ragatz, L.J. *The Fall of the Planter Class in the British Caribbean 1763–1833*. Octagon, 1971.
Reece, J.E., and C.G. Clark-Hunt. *Barbados Diocesan History*. London: The West India Committee, 1925.
Schomburgk, R.H. *The History of Barbados*. London: Longman, 1847.
Stephen, L. (ed.). *Dictionary of National Biography*, Vol. XI. London: Smith, Elder and Co., n.d.

## ADDITIONAL READING

Beckles, H. *Great House Rules: Landless Emancipation and Workers' Protest in Barbados, 1838–1938*. Kingston: Ian Randle, 2004.

Draper, N. *The Price of Emancipation: Slave-ownership, Compensation and British Society at the End of Slavery*. Cambridge: Cambridge University Press, 2009.

Frey, S.R., and B. Wood, eds. *From Slavery to Emancipation in the Atlantic World*. London: Cass, 1999.

Harmer, H.J.P. *The Longman Companion to Slavery, Emancipation and Civil Rights*. London: Longman, 2000.

Heuman, G. *The Routledge History of Slavery*. London: Routledge, 2010.

Hochschild, A. *Bury the Chains: The British Struggle to Abolish Slavery*. London: Macmillan, 2005.

Jacob, W.M. *The Making of the Anglican Church Worldwide*. London: SPCK, 1997.

Minter, R.A. *Episcopacy without Episcopate: The Church of England in Jamaica before 1824*. Upton-upon-Severn: R.A. Minter, 1990.

Temperley, H. (ed.). After Slavery: Emancipation and its Discontents London: Cass, 2000.

Walvin, James. *Black Ivory: Slavery in the British Empire*. Oxford: Blackwell, 2001.

## ARTICLES

The Lucas Manuscript: 'The Commission of Surrogate of the Bishop of London in Barbados', *The Journal of the Barbados Museum and Historical Society*, Vol. XV, No. 4.

B. Hill, 'The Coleridge Chapels of Ease', *The Journal of the Barbados Museum and Historical Society*, Vol. XXXVI, No. 1, 1979.

J.T. Gilmore, 'The Rev. William Harte and Attitudes to Slavery in Early Nineteenth-Century Barbados', *The Journal of Ecclesiastical History*, Vol. 30, No. 4, October 1979.

## SPCK REPORTS (BOUND), SPCK ARCHIVES

Copy of Treasury Minute, 6 October 1826, CO 28/146, PRO X/K 1520.
SPCK Report, 1821, 1826, 1827, 1828, 1829, 1835, 1836, 1837

## MANUSCRIPTS

The Lucas Manuscript, 'The Commission of Surrogate of the Bishop of London in Barbados'. (See under 'Articles'.)
The Lucas Manuscript, Vol. 2.
The Lucas Manuscript, Vol. 3, 15 July 1718.
The Lucas Manuscript, Vol. 15.

## NEWSPAPERS

*The Barbadian*, 28 January 1825, BMHS; 1 February 1825, BMHS; 11 February 1825; 14 February 1825, BMHS; 18 February 1825; 8 March 1825; 11 March 1825; 18 March 1825; 10 September 1830; 16 December 1835; 21 March 1838
*Oxford Herald*. 'Miscellanea', in *Sermons and Tracts*. (See below.)
*Christian Remembrancer*, Vol. VI, 1828; Vol. X, 1828, British Museum; Vol. XI, 1829, British Museum

## LETTERS AND DOCUMENTS IN ARCHIVES

Hall's Laws (BMHS)
Fulham Papers, Vol. 2 (BMHS)
'Bishop's Document Book 1824-1849', Barbados Department of Archives, Vol. 1.
Table of Returns 1841. USPG Archives, London.
Statement of Funds. USPG Archives, London.
Replies to Questions Addressed to the Clergy of the Diocese of Barbados and the Leeward Islands, up to December 31, 1828, USPG Archives.
Four letters from W.H. Coleridge to Rev. John Keble, Oriel College, 1823-1846. The Archives, Keble College, Oxford.
Extracts from a Notebook of the Rt. Rev. W.H. Coleridge, Bishop of Barbados, on his first tour of his Diocese, 1825. Warren Alleyne Collection, Barbados.
F.G. Coleridge to John Keble. 'Coleridge Letters' (R131-142), 134. The Archives, Keble College, Oxford.
Letter from W.H. Coleridge to SPG, 25 September 1830. Barbados (Diocesan) 1824-1846. USPG Archives.
*Sermons and Tracts*. Bodleian, Oxford (bound copy).
Coleridge to Bathurst, and Memorial of the Church... HM Treasury, 4 May 1825, CO 28/146, PRO 7096.

*Note*: USPG material is in a box entitled 'Barbados (Diocesan)'.

## OTHER

Historical Register of the University of Oxford. Oxford, 1900.
Ecclesiastical Calendar of the Diocese of Barbados and the Leeward Islands. Bridgetown, Barbados, 1839. Bodleian.

# INDEX

Abolitionist movement, 4–5, 43
Act for the Abolition of Slavery, 58
Adam, Rev., 10
African customs
    arbour institutions, ix
    as challenge to Church ministry, xviii
    and Christian ministry, 63, 68–69
    funerals, 75–76
All Saints Parish Church, 3, 16
Alleyne, Abel, 72
Alleyne, James Holder, 11
Als, Rev. W., 106n12
amelioration policy
    and education, xviii, 62
    and emancipation, 4–6, 77–79
    role of the Church in, xvii–xviii, 5–6, 8
Anglican Black leadership, development of, viii–ix
Anglican Divines, 64–65
Antigua, 8, 9, 31, 87
Antigua, Archdeaconry of, 30
Anton, J.A., 39
Apostolic Succession, 64
Apprenticeship system
    education programme, 55, 73
    and emancipation, 79–80
    termination of, 81–84
arbour institutions, ix
Archdeacons, appointment and consecration of, 29–30, 87

Archer, Edward J., 59–60
Asylum for the Coloured, 85
Austin, Rev. William Piercy, xviii, 30, 87

Baker, Rev. J.C., 31
baptism, 42, 60, 63, 69–70, 92
*Barbadian* (newspaper)
    on arrival of Bishop Coleridge, 9–11
    on opening of Codrington College, 38–39
    pew-rental controversy, 23–24
Barbados. *See also* colonial governments
    conflict of duties between Bishop and Governor, 12–14
    Henry Warde, Governor, 16
    Kendall as Governor, 3
    Lionel Smith, Governor, 20
    public education, at beginning of Coleridge episcopate, 49–50
    University of the West Indies, Cave Hill, x
Barbados, Archdeaconry of, 30
Barbados and the Leeward Islands, Diocese of
    1825 accommodation, 15–16
    creation of, 6, 8, 102n9
    division of, 87–88
    Rural Deans, 28, 31

Barbados and the Leeward Islands, See of, xvii–xviii, 1, 2–4, 6
Barbados Society for the Education of the Poor, 54
Barclay, J.A., 39
Barrow, John, 17, 60
Barrow, Rev. T.F., 46
Barrow, R.H., 40
Bascom, J.A., 40
Bascom, James Sarsfield, 81
Bathurst, Lord, 9
Bathurst Dispatches, 6
Beckles, J.A., 16
Beckles, W.A., 40
Bell, Andrew, 5
Berbice, 30, 31
'Bishop's Sketch Book', 22
Black Anglican Celebration for the Decade, xiii
Black people
  African customs of, ix, xviii, 63, 68–69, 75–76, 92
  Anglican Black leadership, development of, viii–ix
  baptism, right of, 42, 60, 63, 69–70, 92
  class distinction in church seating, 23, 71, 91
  Codrington Trust Estates education model, 56–57
  education, provision for, 49–50, 57–59
  and Holy Communion, 71
  Negro Education Grant, 61
Black theology, ix, x–xi, xii–xiv
Bolton, Rev., 10
Bowcher Clarke, R., 46
Boyle, Robert, 5
Brathwaite, F.R., 39
Brathwaite, J., 16

Brathwaite, Rev. Samuel Rous Moe, 41
Bray, Thomas, 64
Britain
  Abolitionist movement, 4–5
  Afro-Caribbean post-war migration, xii–xiv
  amelioration policy, xvii–xviii, 5–6, 8
  Bathurst Dispatches, 6
  Canning Resolutions, 4, 6
  clergy, remuneration of, 8, 9, 12, 28–29, 44–46, 97
  early colonial religious policy, 1–2
  grant to 'Church Building Fund', 18
  on jurisdiction of colonial Bishops, 12–14
  'Mixed Fund', 46, 60
  post-war decolonisation, xii
  support of Black education, 49–50, 57–59
British Guiana, 87
  and Diocese of Barbados and the Leeward Islands, 8, 102n9
  Rev. J.H. Pinder as Commissary, 30, 37
  Rev. W.P. Austin as Ecclesiastical Commissary, 30
  building programme, xvii, 90–91
Chapels of Ease, 18–19, 90
'Church Building Fund', 16–17, 18
  rebuilding of 1831 hurricane damage, 19–21, 90–91
  revenue sources, 17–19, 95

Caldecott, A., 9
Canning Resolutions, 4, 6
Canterbury, Province of, 33

Catechetical Fund, 43–44
catechists, ministry of, 28, 32, 33, 42, 60, 92, 97
Catechists, Order of, 43–44
Central Schools, 50, 51, 54, 61, 106n12
Chapel of St. Aidan, 22
Chapels of Ease, 98–99
    All Saints, 15, 19
    architectural style of, 22
    building programme, 18–19, 21, 90, 91
    Codrington College Chapel, 15
    Holy Trinity, 19, 22
    Mortuary Chapel, 22
    Society Chapel, 15, 19
    St. Bartholomew, 19
    St. Luke, 19, 20
    St. Mark, 19, 22
    St. Matthew, 19, 20
    St. Paul, 19, 20, 22
Chapel-Schools, 22, 26, 60, 91, 98–99
Charity Schools, 53, 60
Checkley, Rev. J., 31
Christ Church Parish Church, 16
Christ Church, Parish of, 18, 19, 60, 106n12
Christian Faith Society, 61
'Church Building Fund', 16–17
    revenue sources, 17–18
Church Misionary Society, 53
Church of England. *See also* Colonial Church
    *An Amazing Journey* (Gordon-Carter), xii–xiii
    Apostolic Succession, 63–64
    Board for Social Responsibility, xii
    and canonical obedience, 33
    Clerical Library, 64–65
    colonial clergy, remuneration of, 8, 9, 12, 28–29, 44–46, 97
    colonial jurisdiction of Bishop of London, xvii, 2–4, 12–14
    colonial mission of, xviii
    and colonial policy, 1–2
    Decade of Evangelism, xiii
    Diocese of Barbados and the Leeward Islands, 8, 102n9
    Episcopacy of, 63–64
    jurisdiction of colonial Bishops, xvii, 2–4, 12–14
    Oxford Movement, 64
    Race, Pluralism and Community Group, xii
    Race Relations Field Officers, xii
    reception of Afro-Caribbean migrants, xii–xiv
    and the Reformation, 64
    role of in amelioration policy, xvii–xviii, 5–6, 8
clandestine marriages, 74
Clarke, F., 17
Clarke, Forster, 39, 72, 78, 79
Clarke, Robert Bowcher, 81–82
class distinctions, church seating arrangements, 18, 23–26
clergy, 96–97
    and Chapels of Ease, 21
    discipline of communicants, 70–71
    as educators, 52
    filling of vacancies, 12–13
    financial remuneration, 8, 9, 12, 28–29, 44–46, 97
    increase in numbers of, xviii, 31, 41–42, 106n12
    leaves of absence, 46
    local clergy, training of, xvii, 28, 34–36, 41, 91–92
    overseas recruitment of, 28, 33–34, 91

pastoral care. *See* pastoral care
preferment, question of, 33–34
provision for widows and children, 46–47
scriptural study, importance of, 64–65
visiting, and pastoral care, 2, 63, 66–67
Codrington, Christopher, bequest of, 5, 34–36, 101n19
Codrington, William, 35
Codrington College, 106n12
    academic affiliations, 61–62, 92
    Chapel of Ease, 15
    Commoners, 40, 107n33
    enrolment, 40–42
    first examination results, 39–40
    Foundation Scholars, 36, 37–38, 39, 107n33
    Goodridge, principalship of, xi
    and Harrison's Free School, 51
    local clergy, training of, 28, 34–36, 40–41, 91–92
    opening ceremony, 38–39
    post-hurricane rebuilding programme, 41
    readers, ministry of, 28, 42–43
    re-organisation of, xvii–xviii, 28, 31, 36–38, 61–62, 91–92
    student body, 37–38, 39–40
    theological instruction, establishment of, 36–38
Codrington Grammar School, 36, 61
Codrington Trust Estates, 31, 106n12
    allotment system, 78–79, 80–81, 93
    bequest to Society for the Propagation of the Gospel in Foreign Parts, 34–36
    as education model, 56–57
    gradual emancipation plan, 77–79, 93
    labour expense post-emancipation, 80
    'located labour' system, 84, 93
    marriage among enslaved people, 72–73
    Society Chapel, 15
    Society for the Propagation of the Gospel in Foreign Parts, as trustee, 5–6, 101n19
    task labour, 78
    termination of Apprenticeship, 82–84
Coleridge, Edward, and St. Augustine's missionary college, 88–90
Coleridge, Luke Herman, 7
Coleridge, Rev. George, 7
Coleridge, William Hart (Bishop of Barbados and the Leeward Islands)
    administrative system, xvii–xviii
    building programme, xvii, 16–17, 18–21, 90–91
    Colonial Churches, mission of, xviii
    consecration of in Barbados, 9–11
    delegation of authority, 28–31, 91
    education policy, 50–52, 53–56
    on emancipation, 86
    financial remuneration, 8, 9
    'Gibraltar' (Coleridge residence), 11
    on jurisdiction as Bishop, 12
    marriage of, 10, 102–03n15
    as moderniser, vii–viii
    nomination of as Bishop of Barbados and Leeward Islands, 7–9
    return to England, 87
    and Society for Promoting Christian Knowledge, 7

Index    123

on spiritual welfare of British
    Empire, 87–88
at St. Andrew's (Holborn), 7, 8
on state of education (1830),
    56–57
view of ordination, 63–64
as Warden, St. Augustine's
    missionary college, xviii
youth and education, 7
'Coleridge Romantic Gothic Revival
    Style', 22
Colonial Church. See also Church of
    England
    Bishop as 'full Ordinary', 12
    catechists, 28
    'Church Building Fund', 16–17
    class stratification within, 23, 71, 91
    clergy vacancies, filling of, 12–13
    financial provision, 1, 4, 6
    as jurisdiction of Bishop of
        London, xvii
    jurisdiction of colonial Bishops,
        12–14
    pew rental system, 15, 17–18,
        23–26, 91
    readers, ministry of, 28
    rebuilding of 1831 hurricane
        damage, 19–21
    religious instruction, and public
        education, 5–6, 32–33, 35,
        49–50, 56, 57, 65
    role of in evangelisation and
        amelioration, xvii–xviii
    spiritual vs. civil education, 54
colonial governments
    building programme, financial
        support, 18
    clergy vacancies, filling of, 12–13
    commissaries, ecclesiastic author-
        ity of, 2–4

education, support of, 57–59, 60
elections in parish churches, 26
Governor Lowther, 3, 4
role of Governor as 'Ordinary',
    1–3, 8, 90
Coloured people
    class distinction in church seating,
        23, 25
    education, provision for, 49–50,
        55–56
    Old Church Yard School, 49, 53
Combermere, Lord, and Central
    Schools, 50, 54
Combermere School, 50, 61
commissaries, ecclesiastic authority
    of, 2–4
Common Gaol, reforms to, 85–86
communicants, discipline of, 70–71
Compton, Bishop, 2
concubinage, xviii, 63, 92
Confirmation, preparation for, 56
congregational singing, 68, 89
Connecticut, 1
Continental Protestants, 63–64
Coppage, Captain, 83
Coulthurst, M., 17
Council of Churches for Britain and
    Ireland
    Community and Race Relations
        Unit, xiii
Coventry, Mr., 10
Cranmer, Thomas, 64
Cryer (commissary), 4
Culpepper, Rev. G.P., 45
Cummins, H.S., 17
Cummins, Rev. C.C., 45
Cummins, Rev. George, 31
Cutting, John, 85

Daily Meal Society, 65–66

Davis, Rev. Daniel Gateward, xviii,
    31, 87
Deane (Church Building Fund), 17
Demerara, 30
Diocesan Committee, 54, 55
Dissenters, 5
Doctors Commons, on preferment, 9,
    33–34
Dominica, 8, 30
Drax, Henry, 50

education. *See also* schools; Sunday
    Schools
  at beginning of Coleridge episcopate, 49–50
  Charity Schools, 53
  Codrington Trust Estates model
    of, 56–57
  co-education, 54
  of Coloured people, 49, 53–56
  consolidation and centralisation
    of, 51–52, 92
  district schools, establishment of,
    49–50
  funding, 50, 51, 52, 53, 59, 60–61
  girls curriculum, 50, 56, 60
  National Schools for teacher-training, 58–59
  Negro Education Grant, 61
  oversight of schools by clergy, 65
  and religious instruction, 5–6,
    32–33, 35, 49–50, 56, 57, 65
  role of in amelioration policy,
    xviii, 62
  state of in 1830, 56–57
  teacher qualifications, 50, 52
  teacher salaries, 54, 60–61, 97
  unordained teachers, 59–60
Eliot, Rev. Edward (Archdeacon of
    Barbados), 30

Elizabeth II, Queen, xiv
emancipation
  Act for the Abolition of Slavery,
    58
  and amelioration policy, 4–6, 77–79
  Coleridge on, 86
  compensation to planters, 80
  and monogamous marriage, 73
  post-emancipation education programme, 57–59
  termination of Apprenticeship,
    81–84
Emancipation Act, 79–80
enslaved people
  African customs of, ix, xviii, 63,
    68–69, 75–76
  allotment system, 78–79, 80–81
  baptism, 42, 60, 63, 69–70, 92
  catechists, ministry of, 42, 43–44
  class distinction in church seating,
    23, 25
  education of, xviii, 53, 54, 55
  emancipation of, 4, 73
  gradual emancipation plan, 77–79
  marriage between, 71–73
  post-emancipation education programme, 57–59
  punishment, regulation of, 6, 77,
    78
  readers, ministry of, 28, 42–43
  reading instruction, 56, 57
  religious instruction, 5–6, 32–33,
    35, 56, 57, 65
  role of the Church in amelioration,
    4–6
  visiting of by clergy, 66–67
Episcopacy of Church of England,
    63–64
Essequibo, 30

Estate Schools, 56–57, 60, 65
evangelisation
  and education, 62
  role of the Church in amelioration, xvii–xviii
Evening Schools, 60
Eversley, W., 17
Eversley, W., Esq., 17

Fitzpatrick, Nathaniel, 45, 60
Fox, William, 5
Friendly Societies, 84
Froude, Rev. Richard Hurrell, 29
funerals, 63, 75–76

Garland, J.N., 40
Garnett, Rev. William, 10, 11, 16, 31, 106n12
General Hospital, opening of, 85
General Synod Board of Mission, xiii
Gibraltar' (Coleridge residence), 11
Gibraltar, Bishop of, 87
Gibson, Bishop Edmund, 3
Gill, Rev. C.C., 60
Gill, W., 16
Gittens, D., 40
Gittens, J.A., 40
Gittens, Rev. J.H., 16, 31, 40
Glenelg, Lord, 57, 58, 59
*Globe* (newspaper)
  conflict over Harte's equality sermon, 32–33
Goddard, Rev., 10
Goodridge, Rt. Rev. Sehon S.
  academic affiliations, viii, x
  as activist, viii
  on Bishop Coleridge as moderniser, vii–viii
  as Bishop of the Windward Islands, x, xiv
  on Black theology, ix, x–xi, xii–xiv
  on British culture in West Indies, ix
  Codrington College, principalship, xi
  marriage, viii
  as Royal Chaplain, xiv
  sermons, x–xi
  Simon of Cyrene Theological Institute, x, xiii
  at University of the West Indies, Cave Hill, xi–xii
  at University of West Indies, Mona, viii–ix, x, xi
  written works, vii
Gordon, William, 3, 4
Gordon-Carter, Glynne, xii–xiii
Gothic Revival architecture, 22
Grant, F.B., 40
Grenada, 8, 30, 31
Grenada Truth and Reconciliation Commission, xiv
Grenville, Lord, 5

Hall, Rev. Henry Newton Gage, 41
Hamden, R., 16
Harrison, Thomas, 50–51
Harrison College, 61
Harrison's Free School, 50–51, 61
Hart, Richard, 7
Harte, Rev. William M., 31–33, 45, 47, 85, 106n12
  and Sabbath observance, 68–69
Haynes, General, 51
Haynes, R., 16
Higginson (Church Building Fund), 17
Hinds, G.M., 17
Hinds, Rev. W.P., 31, 52, 106n12
Hinkson (manager, Codrington Estates), 78

Hobson, J., 40
Holberton, Rev. Robert, 31
Holt, Rev. Joseph, 43
Holy Communion, 63, 71
Horton, J.W., 9
Hume, David, xiii
Hurricane Subscription Fund, 19, 95

Infant Schools, 60
Inter-Anglican Theological and
　Doctrinal Commission, viii
Irvine, Rev. Dr. Charles, 4

Jackson, Rev. W.M., 59
Jackson, W.W., 39, 42
Jamaica
　decolonisation movement, xi, xii
　United Theological College of the
　　West Indies, x
Jamaica, Diocese of, 6, 8, 46, 55, 90
Jamaica, Island Council of
　St. Peter's theological college, 48
Jamaica, See of
　colonial jurisdiction of Bishop of
　　London, 2–3
　creation of, 1, 6
　evangelisation, and amelioration
　　policy, xvii–xviii
Jemmett, G., 17
Jones, Rev. Henry, 41

Keble, Rev. John, 29, 48, 64, 88,
　105n2
Kendall, James, 3
King, A., 17
King, Bishop, 2
King, Rev. R.F., 46, 106n12
King, Thomas, 80, 82, 83, 84
Knight, Rt. Rev. Alan John, xi

Ladies Branch Association for the
　Education of Female Children of the
　Coloured Poor in the Principles of
　the Established Church of England,
　54, 55–56
Lambeth Conference
　Decade of Evangelism, xiii
　Human Rights resolutions, xiv
Laud, Archbishop, 2
leaves of absence, 46
Letters Patent
　Archdeacons, appointment of, 29–30
　and Diocese of Barbados and the
　　Leeward Islands, 8, 30, 33,
　　102n9
　jurisdiction of colonial Bishops,
　　14, 90
Lipscomb, Rt. Rev. Christopher
　as Bishop, Diocese of Jamaica, 8,
　　46, 55, 90
　consecration of in Barbados, 10
Little St. Joseph Chapel School, 22
Lodge School, 61
London, Bishop of
　appointment of Coleridge as
　　Bishop, 7–9
　colonial ecclesiastical jurisdiction
　　of, xvii, 2–4, 12–14
Lords Committee of Trade and
　Plantations, 2–3
Lord's Supper, 70–71
Lovell, Rev. E., 45
Lowther, Governor, 3, 4
Lucas, N., 16
Luggar, Lieutenant, 53
Lushington, Stephen, on preferment,
　33–34

Manross, W.W., 1
manumissions

Codrington Trust Estates, 77
restrictions on, 6
marriage, 63
  banns and licences, 74
  clandestine marriages, 74
  directions to clergy, 73–74
  encouragement of among enslaved people, 6, 72–73
  between enslaved people, 33, 71–73
  monogamy, and policy of gradualism, 72, 73, 92
  by 'other religious teachers', 74–75
  separation, and re-marriage, 75
Massiah, Mr., St. Peter's Benevolent School, 60
Masters and Servants Act (1840), 84
Maycock, John Dotten, 17, 37
Maynard, Rev. G.F., 106n12
Medical Dispensary Society, 85
Methodist Church, 64
  Negro Education Grant, 61
Mills, 40
Mixed Fund, 46, 60
Montserrat, 8, 30
Moravian Church, 64
  marriages by, 74–75
  Negro Education Grant, 61
Morle, Mr., 61
Musson, S.P., 40

National Schools for teacher-training, 58–59, 60
Neblett, Rev. James, 31
Negro Education Grant, 61
Nevis, 8, 30
Newsam, C.A., 61
Nicholson, Rev. Mark, 32
Nurse, Bryan Taylor, 34

obeah, xviii, 63, 68, 75, 92
Orderson, Rev. T.H., 106n12
Oxford Movement, 64
Oxley, W., 17

Packer, Rev. John, 31, 37–38, 50, 53, 72, 106n12
parish churches, Barbados, 98–99
  1825 accommodation, 15–16
  accommodation, increases in, 22–23, 25–26
  All Saints Parish Church, 3, 16
  attendance, 26–27
  Christ Church, 16
  class distinctions in, 18, 23–26
  'Coleridge Romantic Gothic Revival Style', 22
  elections in, 26
  pew rental system, 15, 23–26
  rebuilding of 1831 hurricane damage, 19–21
  St. Andrew, 16, 26
  St. George, 16
  St. James, 16
  St. John, 16, 22, 31
  St. Joseph, 16, 22
  St. Lucy, 16
  St. Mary's, 17–18, 26
  St. Michael's Cathedral, 16, 20, 26
  St. Michael's Church, 10
  St. Paul's, 26
  St. Peter, 16, 31
  St. Philip, 16, 22
  St. Thomas, 16
parishes
  and Chapels of Ease, 21
  Christ Church, 18, 19, 49, 60, 106n12
  post-hurricane rebuilding programme, 19–21

St. Andrew, 20, 49, 106n12
St. George, 19, 20, 49, 106n12
St. James, 18, 20, 49, 106n12
St. John, 19, 22, 49, 106n12
St. Joseph, 31, 32, 49, 106n12
St. Lucy, 32, 49, 60, 106n12
St. Mary's, 17
St. Michael, 4, 16–17, 19, 20, 22, 49, 106n12
St. Peter, 3, 15, 31, 49, 60
St. Philip, 18, 19, 49, 106n12
St. Thomas, 18, 49, 106n12
Parkinson, Rev. H., 106n12
Parliamentary Hurricane Fund, 19–21
Parochial Boys' School, 60
Parochial Girls' School, 60
Parry, Rev. Thomas, xviii, 9, 10, 30, 40, 60, 85, 87
Pascoe, C.F., 1, 8
pastoral care
 and African customs, xviii, 63, 68–69, 75–76, 92
 and amelioration policy, xviii
 of children, 65–66
 clergy, duties of, 63
 congregational singing, 68
 funerals, 75–76
 preaching, 67–68
 of the sick, 66–67
 visiting, 2, 63, 66–67
Paterson, Rev., 10
Payne, Rev. W.M., 23, 106n12
Pearn, J.M., 39
pew rental system, 15, 17–18, 91
 controversy over, 23–26
Pilgrim, Rev. J.F., 106n12
Pinder, Rev. John Hothersall
 Codrington College principalship, 29, 41
 as Codrington Estates chaplain, 5, 37, 72
 as Commissary to British Guiana, 30
Pinder, Rev. W.L., 106n12
Pine Estate, 11
polygamy, xviii, 63, 71–72, 73, 92
Pope, Rev. Mr. (Archdeacon of Jamaica), 10
Porteus, Bishop Beilby, 5
post-hurricane rebuilding programme, 19–21
preaching, and pastoral care, 67–68
prisoners, conditions for, 85–86
private subscriptions, building programme, 18
public education. See education
punishment, of enslaved people, 6, 77, 78

Queen's College, 61

racial prejudice, Church response to, xii–xiv
Ragatz, L.J., 5
readers, ministry of, 28, 42–43, 92
Redwar, Rev. T.R., 31, 40
religious instruction, 5–6, 32–33, 35, 49–50, 56, 57, 65
Rhode Island, 1
Ribbitz's Ground, 18
Robin, Jack, 78
Romantic Gothic Revival architecture, 22, 90
Rural Deans, 28, 31, 91

Sabbath breaking, xviii, 68–69
Saint Christopher, 8, 30
Saint Lucia, 8, 30
Saint Vincent, 8, 30

Schomburgk, R.H., 56
schools. *See also* education; Sunday Schools
   attendance levels, 57, 60
   at beginning of Coleridge episcopate, 49–50
   Central District School, 51–52
   Chapel-Schools, 22, 26, 60, 91
   Charity Schools, 53
   curriculum, 50, 56, 60
   development of, 53–56
   district schools, establishment of, 49–50
   Estate Schools, 56–57, 60, 65
   Evening Schools, 60
   funding, 50, 51, 52, 53, 59, 60–61
   Infant Schools, 60
   National Schools for teacher-training, 60
   oversight of by clergy, 65
   post-emancipation education programme, 57–59, 60
Scott (Church Building Fund), 17
Scottish Presbyterians, 63–64
Sealy, G.F., 40
Sealy, Rev. W.D., 60
Selwyn, George Augustus (Bishop of New Zealand), 88
Sherlock, Bishop Thomas, 3
Simon of Cyrene Theological Institute, x, xiii
Skeete, K.B., 39
slavery
   abolition of, 4–5
   amelioration policy, 4–6
Smith, Edward Parris, 36, 37
Smith, Sir Lionel, 20
social reforms post-emancipation, xviii
   Friendly Societies, 84

'located labour' system, 84
prisoners, conditions for, 85–86
Society for Promoting Christian Knowledge (SPCK)
   building programme, financial support, 18
   clergy, remuneration of, 46
   clerical libraries, 64–65
   Coleridge as Secretary, 7
   financial support, 55
   National School Books, 55
   post-hurricane rebuilding programme, 41
   public education, support of, 54–55
Society for the Conversion and Religious Instruction and Education of the Negro Slaves in the British West Indian Islands, 5
Society for the Conversion of Blacks, 43–44
Society for the Propagation of the Gospel in Foreign Parts (SPG)
   allotment system, 78–79
   building programme, financial support, 18
   catechists, ministry of, 43–44
   clergy, remuneration of, 46
   Codrington bequest, 5, 101n19
   on Codrington College, 36–37
   Codrington Estates, role of as trustee, 5–6, 101n19
   creation of West Indian Sees, 1
   gradual emancipation plan, 77–79
   labour expense post-emancipation, 80
   marriage among enslaved people, 72–73
   post-hurricane rebuilding programme, 41

social reforms post-emancipation, 84–85
termination of Apprenticeship, 82–84
Society for the Relief of the Widows and Fatherless Children of Clergymen in the Diocese of Barbados and the Leeward Islands', 46–47
St. Alban Chapel-School, 22
St. Andrew Parish Church, 16
St. Andrew, Parish of, 106n12
  rebuilding of 1831 hurricane damage, 19–21
  schools, 49
St. Andrew's Parish Church, 16, 26
St. Augustine's, Canterbury (missionary college), xviii
St. Barnabas Chapel-School, 22
St. Catherine Chapel-School, 22
St. Christopher's, 31
St. David Chapel-School, 22
St. George, Parish of, 106n12
  rebuilding of 1831 hurricane damage, 19–21
  schools, 49
St. Luke, Chapel of Ease, 19
St. George's Parish Church, 16
St. Giles Chapel-School, 22
St. James Parish Church, 16
St. James, Parish of, 18, 106n12
rebuilding of 1831 hurricane damage, 19–21
  schools, 49
St. John, Parish of, 106n12
  Mortuary Chapel, 22
  schools, 49
  St. Mark, Chapel of Ease, 19
St. John's Parish Church, 16, 22, 31
St. Joseph Parish Church, 22

St. Joseph, Parish of, 31, 32, 49, 106n12
St. Joseph's Parish Church, 16
St. Lawrence Chapel-School, 22
St. Lucy, Parish of, 32, 49, 60, 106n12
St. Lucy's Church, 16
St. Martin Chapel-School, 22
St. Mary's Church, 17–18, 26
St. Mary's, Parish of, 17
St. Matthias Chapel-School, 22
St. Michael, Parish of, 16–17, 106n12
  commissaries, 4
  rebuilding of 1831 hurricane damage, 19–21
  schools, 49, 53
  St. Matthew, Chapel of Ease, 19
  St. Paul, Chapel of Ease, 19, 22
St. Michael's Cathedral, 16, 20, 26
St. Michael's Parish Church, 10
St. Patrick Chapel-School, 22
St. Paul's Church, 26
St. Peter Parish Church, 16, 31
St. Peter, Parish of, 3, 15, 31
  Central District School, 51–52
  schools, 49, 60
St. Peter's Benevolent School, 60
St. Philip Parish Church, 16, 22
St. Philip, Parish of, 18, 49, 106n12
Holy Trinity, Chapel of Ease, 19
St. Saviour Chapel-School, 22
St. Simon Chapel-School, 22, 26
St. Swithin Chapel-School, 22
St. Thomas Parish Church, 16
St. Thomas, Parish of, 18, 49, 106n12
St. Vincent, 31
stamp duty, and Archdeaconries, 29–30
Stanley, Lord, 79

Sterling, Rev. John, post-emancipation education programme, 58–59
Sunday markets, 6, 63, 69
Sunday Schools, 33, 60
    Codrington Estates, 5
    for enslaved people, 56, 57
    readers, ministry of, 28, 42–43
superstition, as African custom, 63

task labour, 78
Tasmania, BIshop of, 87
teacher-catechists, 45
Thomas, Richard Caddy, 34
Tobago, 8, 30
Trinidad, 8, 30, 31
Trotman, Donald, xiv
Tutu, Archbishop Desmond, xiv

United Theological College of the West Indies, x, xi
University of the West Indies, Cave Hill, x, xi–xii
University of the West Indies, Mona, viii–ix, x, xi

Virgin Islands, 8, 30
Virginia Company, 2
visiting, and pastoral care, 2, 63, 66–67

Walker, Rev. William, 3
Warde, Sir Henry, 16
Watts, Rev. Thomas, 78, 79
Wesleyan chapels, architecture of, 22
Wesleyan missionaries, 74–75
West, Rev. J.K., 45
West India Building Fund, 18
West Indies
    commissaries, 2–4
    ecclesiastic authority of Bishop of London, 2–4
    National Schools for teacher-training, 58–59
White population
    class distinctions among, 52
    education of poor White children, 49, 51
    and Holy Communion, 71
Wilberforce, William, 5, 79
Windward Islands, Bishop of, x, xiv

www.ingramcontent.com/pod-product-compliance
Lightning Source LLC
Chambersburg PA
CBHW020853160426
43192CB00007B/905